Brion Gardner

By

Eka Okonmkpaeto

On the Occasion of

Retirement

Date

July 6, 2001

All I Have Needed

A 40-DAY DEVOTIONAL JOURNEY

Elva Minette Martin

BARBOUR
PUBLISHING, INC.
Uhrichsville, Ohio

DEDICATION

To Randi Minette Jewell,
my first granddaughter, my namesake,
and always a shining jewel in my heart.
Thank you, Nette, for ever being content
in whatever circumstance
and with whatever you have.
Love you, Nana Minette

© 2001 by Elva Minette Martin

ISBN 1-58660-136-9

All Scripture quotations, unless otherwise noted, are taken from the King James Version of the Bible.

Scripture quotations marked NKJV are taken from the New King James Version. Copyright © 1979, 1980, 1982 by Thomas Nelson, Inc. Used by permission. All rights reserved.

Scripture quotations marked AMPLIFIED are from the Amplified New Testament, © 1954, 1958, 1987 by the Lockman Foundation. Used by permission.

Published by Barbour Publishing, Inc., P.O. Box 719, Uhrichsville, Ohio 44683 http://www.barbourbooks.com

Member of the
Evangelical Christian
Publishers Association

Printed in the United States of America.

Contents

THE HEARTBEAT OF GOD

"My Father, God, I need. . ." Right there the Lord stopped me as I prayed. He asked, "What do you need this minute?"

It took scarcely a breath to reply, "Well, I don't actually need one thing at this moment, but later on. . .tomorrow. . .next month. . ."

"Child, leave the next hour, the rest of the day, yes, the rest of your life to My care. I will never fail to supply all you need, just at the moment you need it."

That was God's answer. I knew I should not ask, "How?" There was no urgency to know when. I really did not need a single thing at that moment —except the realization that I could wait on my God, trust Him implicitly, and not fret. I needed to go on with my life, doing only and all He would tell me to do. I needed to let God be my God.

"Lord, I need to trust You more. That is exactly what You are allowing me room to do, isn't it?"

He held me tenderly in His everlasting arms. It was worth the entire world and everything in it to feel the heartbeat of my Father and look up into the face of God.

FAITH IS. . .

What do I need today? I can go ahead and list each item: faith, security, hope, wisdom, direction, peace, health, strength, friends, money, time. . .

Now, what do I need today that my heavenly Father cannot or will not provide? He promised all I need. There are no limitations on the word *all*. It stands alone in perfect completeness. *All*. And it is mine through faith.

"Now faith is the substance (the confirmation, the title-deed) of the things we hope for, being the proof of things we do not see and the conviction of their reality" (Hebrews 1:1 AMPLIFIED). This does not mean mindlessness, but rather freedom from worry about matters I cannot control. It is an assurance, quiet and contented, and is an evidence that God is. It is proof that His Word is living truth, effective in my heart and in my life because I believe.

What proof can I claim, when I do not yet have the actual item at hand? I claim God's Word, assert that if God says it is mine, it is. Faith is contentment with what I have now, and quiet expectancy of having what I may need in a moment or a day or a year. It is mine by title-deed; my name is on the contract and it will be available for my use at the exact moment I need it.

Faith is trusting my future, from now to the next moment and to forever, unto my Heavenly Father's wisdom. Faith lived out is visible evidence of things not seen!

WHY TAKE THOUGHT?

Why take ye thought?
Doth He not clothe the lily?
Doth He not feed the bird?
Everything that God has made
Is sustained through His Word.

So why take thought?
Hath He not clothed thee fine and shod?
Hath the body without food ever gone?
Try to recall one unquenched need
Through all thy lifetime long.

Then why anxiety or unrest?
Why fear, or even concern?
Has immutable God transformed?
What He has eternally promised
Will He not forever perform?

Then why take thought?
Why not cease struggling with the oars
While heading across life's sea?
For Sovereign God has whispered,
"Leave all your needs with Me."

PART 1

"THE WORD OF THE LORD CAME"

1 KINGS 16:29–17:16

And Elijah the Tishbite, who was of the inhabitants of Gilead, said unto Ahab, As the LORD God of Israel liveth, before whom I stand, there shall not be dew nor rain these years, but according to my word. And the word of the LORD came unto him, saying, Get thee hence, and turn thee eastward, and hide thyself by the brook Cherith, that is before Jordan. And it shall be, that thou shalt drink of the brook; and I have commanded the ravens to feed thee there.

So he went and did according unto the word of the LORD: for he went and dwelt by the brook Cherith, that is before Jordan. And the ravens brought him bread and flesh in the morning, and bread and flesh in the evening; and he drank of the brook. And it came to pass after a while, that the brook dried up, because there had been no rain in the land.

1 KINGS 17:1–7

1

The King and I

1 Kings 17:1

To the King

> *They are foolish:*
> *for they know not the way of the LORD.*

JEREMIAH 5:4

To Elijah

> *Be not afraid of the king. . .be not afraid of him,*
> *saith the LORD: for I am with you to save you,*
> *and to deliver you from his hand.*

JEREMIAH 42:11

King Ahab had done more to provoke the LORD God to anger than all of the previous kings of Israel. God's prophet Elijah was a man whose heart was yielded to God, whose actions were exemplary, and whose life was carried out in obedience to God to the nth degree. God sent Elijah to deliver a message to King Ahab.

Who was Elijah? Where was he from? What had he been doing before God called him to be His messenger? God's Word is quiet regarding this, except to say that Elijah was from Gilead. Then suddenly Elijah is brought on the scene at the perfect time and in the exact place of God's choosing.

Thus a lowly prophet of God, clothed in camel's skin, was sent to speak to the king of the land.

God hath chosen the foolish things
of the world to confound the wise;
and God hath chosen the weak things of the world
to confound the things which are mighty;
and base things of the world,
and things which are despised, hath God chosen. . .
to bring to nought things that are.
1 CORINTHIANS 1:27–28

God's prophet Elijah stood before that wicked king and spoke: "As the LORD God of Israel liveth, before whom I stand. . ." First he introduced the authority by which he spoke: the LORD God. The LORD is Jehovah, the I AM, the self-existent One, Who gives life to all that lives. The name God signifies the all-powerful One. Then Elijah went on to explain concisely to the king the coming drought:

As the LORD God of Israel liveth,
before whom I stand,
there shall not be dew nor rain these years,
but according to my word.
1 KINGS 17:1

How could a lowly prophet speak this boldly? Because he belonged to the LORD God, took direction from the LORD God, and was upheld by the same LORD God. His God! He had learned unquestioning obedience.

Elijah did not stand in the way of sinners (Psalm 1:1) but in God's sight had clean hands and a pure heart (Psalm 24:4). Then the LORD stood with him to save him (Psalm 109:31). The prophet left Ahab without a hand being laid upon him.

I wonder how many times Elijah had fallen on his face before God in the mountains of Gilead, how many times he had shed tears in a lonely cave. He had learned to know his God! He had learned unquestioning obedience. He stood before God because he was clothed in God's righteousness (or "rightwiseness").

I will speak of thy testimonies also before kings,
and will not be ashamed.
PSALM 119:46

That sounds great, but this is an Old Testament story. It's true, but can it help us today? Definitely yes! God says that everyone is a sinner. If He were to count all our sins, none could stand before Him, but in the New Testament, God explains His free gift of salvation:

The blood of Jesus Christ his Son
cleanseth us from all sin.
1 JOHN 1:7

This is God's gracious gift of salvation to all people, to all who reach out and accept it. Elijah received this salvation by looking ahead to the death of Jesus Christ on the cross, believing Christ would die in his place. We who live after Christ died look back to that same sacrifice for forgiveness of our sins.

God urges us to stand fast in freedom from the power of sin over our lives. He promises to hold us up so we might stand before Himself, the King of Kings, without guilt.

Hold thou me up, and I shall be safe:
and I will have respect unto thy statutes continually.
PSALM 119:117

God enables us to stand firm in our faith before others, too.

Happy are these thy servants,
which stand continually before thee.
1 KINGS 10:8

I wonder if King Ahab, hearing Elijah's prediction of drought, tried to ignore what he heard. I wonder if he thought, *I have wells and water and storehouses full of grains, and houses and lands, and I can do without you, Elijah. I have Baal, the farm god, who gives increase to families, fields, flocks, and herds. He also is the storm god. I will expect Baal's voice to be heard in the thunder, when he brings rain to water my crops. Yes, I can manage without you, Elijah. And I can do without your God, as well.*

Watch out, King Ahab! You may become just as dusty and thirsty as the rest of the people of this land.

—⁓—

2

BREAKFAST
(No Bed Included)

1 KINGS 17:2–3

"Get thee hence, and turn thee eastward, and hide thyself by the brook Cherith" (1 Kings 17:3). This was God's instruction to His prophet Elijah—no explanation, no reason why. Just "Go!"

Humanly speaking, Elijah needed time to prepare. He had a trip to take and a time of seclusion to experience. Most of us would have been frantically buying food and other supplies, packing suitcases, constantly adding to our "to take" list of necessities and desirables.

Elijah heard God's word and simply took God at His word. God did not say to pack. He said, "Go eastward and hide yourself." End of instructions, although God did mention that He would provide food and water.

Elijah heard the instructions and considered

Who was speaking. He would not have entertained the idea if King Ahab had given those commands, but it is obvious he believed God completely, 100 percent, and trusted God's faithfulness. Elijah went, turned, and hid; all that God had told him to do—only what God prescribed—he did. He obeyed "heartily, as to the Lord, and not unto men" (Colossians 3:23).

> *I will hear what God the LORD will speak.*
> PSALM 85:8

Elijah actually went on this journey to camp by a brook without suitcases or enough food in his knapsack. In fact, he did not have any idea how long he would be there. He simply followed God, implicitly trusting God's word. He did what God said to do. How could Elijah step out and follow a way the whole world would consider foolish? He went because of the one Who gave the directive; Elijah trusted God absolutely. Trusting one Who is completely trustworthy is not foolish.

No one can describe the essence of God; that is, just what makes God, God. We would have to be God to understand Him completely, but He reveals Himself to us through His written Word. Going even further, He also revealed Himself to us in the person of Jesus Christ. Jesus said:

He that hath seen me hath seen the Father.
JOHN 14:9

Jesus was God in a body. Humans have seen God with their eyes and touched Him with their hands! Those who companied with Him on earth wrote of Him in the Bible so that we can know Him, too. The Bible is the written Word of God; Jesus is the living Word of God. We can experience a personal relationship with eternal God through His Son, the Lord Jesus Christ!

Elijah was not afraid to obey this Master of the universe. What could there be to fear? God was his God.

Some one thousand years after Elijah unquestioningly followed God's directives, the apostle Paul was in prison, facing martyrdom. He expressed what Elijah might have felt and believed:

God. . .hath saved us,
and called us with an holy calling. . .
according to his own purpose and grace. . . .
For the which cause I also suffer these things:
nevertheless I am not ashamed:
for I know whom I have believed,
and am persuaded that he is able to keep that
which I have committed unto him. . . .
2 TIMOTHY 1:8–9, 12

Elijah's obedience to God did not have its inception at the time he walked into King Ahab's palace to proclaim the coming drought. The Bible does not mention anything about Elijah's parents or life up to the moment recorded in 1 Kings 17:1, except that he was a Tishbite from Gilead. He was then from Tishbe, a town in Gilead. Elijah would have belonged to the tribe of Gad or the half-tribe of Manasseh. Matthew Henry suggests that Israel was sorely wounded, and God sent this balm, Elijah, from Gilead to bring healing to the nation.

We see Elijah as the deliverer of God's message: no rain for some years, except by Elijah's word. It was most likely his practice to obey God's Word, as he fully demonstrated here. He spoke unhesitatingly, fearlessly. He spoke positively, with no embarrassment. It had become his way of life to hear God's voice and carry out God's directions. That's not a bad way to live!

Elijah must have walked with God and been certain that God is faithful and always keeps His word. How else would he dare to walk into the presence of the king of the land and pronounce doom for his entire kingdom? He had to be under authority, or else he was "unwitting" and "a fool."

Elijah could not go wrong by obeying God's word, walking in His revealed will. He wisely trusted and obeyed God unquestioningly.

—⁓—

3

TURN EAST, YOUNG MAN! FACE THE FRONT!

1 KINGS 17:3

God did not simply tell Elijah to go away; He gave specific words regarding direction and destination. The direction was eastward. When the Hebrew people sought a direction, they faced east, so to them the east was the "front." The sun rises in the east. God was not sending Elijah out into darkness! When Elijah turned eastward in obedience, he turned his heart and his face toward God.

When Moses was burdened by the great responsibility of leading the Israelites to the Promised Land, he prayed:

Shew me now thy way, that I may know thee.
EXODUS 33:13

God's answer was:

My presence shall go with thee,
and I will give thee rest.
EXODUS 33:14

God did not send a guide. He did not give a map and lengthy written-out directions. He Himself went with Moses and the Israelites, as He did with Elijah.

Was Elijah breathing a similar petition from his heart? *LORD, I don't know how I can make the journey. Show me Your way; go before me, and go with me. If only You are with me, I know all will be well.*

God does not put us here on earth to live alone and try to glorify Him. He lives here within us, if we invite Him. He carries out through us all that He requires of us.

Does not a teacher, seeing a student turned in his seat to talk to a friend behind, admonish the pupil to turn around and face the front? If he obeys and faces the front, he is facing the teacher, not seeing the distractions around him. Facing the one giving the instructions will help the student to understand the work he will be assigned to do.

God is ever near and presiding over affairs of this life: We may rest in His sovereignty. God's presence gives us rest from sin, confusion, fear, dread, and uncertainty. He also guarantees we will never be all alone in joys or sorrows, in daily duties, in needling necessities or sudden pressured provocations. We need only face the front, to set our hearts eastward, to face the Son of God, to follow all His directions, and do all His bidding.

God tells us of the temple that Solomon built:

The glory of the LORD had filled the house of the LORD.
1 KINGS 8:11

In Ezekiel 44, God describes the temple that will be built during the millennial reign of the Lord Jesus Christ on earth, and the glory of the Lord will enter the house by way of the eastern gate.

Sadly, in today's age of grace, we can only say "Ichabod," which means that the glory has departed, not only from God's temple, but also from His world. As a general rule, we inhabitants of earth today have turned our eyes and hearts to face the temporary things of earth. We look to self-will and self-gratification, to material things and adding to our stockpiles of them. Mark Twain put it succinctly: "Civilization is a limitless multiplication of unnecessary necessities." We look eagerly for recognition of our personal accomplishments. We look to the world, pursuing its pleasures until our energy is expended. We have not time or sinew to be quiet and remember that God is. We have no tears for a lost and dying world of human eternal souls nor the urgency to tell them that there is hope in looking to the Christ of Calvary.

God must look at our nation and our world and weep and plead, "If only you would turn your face to Me!"

It is not too late! He is still waiting, giving lost souls the opportunity to receive the free gift of God —eternal life—giving His children opportunity to bring glory to His name.

God's Word explains that when one believes in the Lord Jesus Christ for forgiveness of sin, Jesus Christ enters and dwells within. As that one opens the heart gate of his or her inner being toward God, He takes him or her into the inner court of His own heart.

The king hath brought me into his chambers. . .
the midst thereof being paved with love. . . .
We will be glad and rejoice in thee,
we will remember thy love more than wine:
the upright love thee.
SONG OF SOLOMON 1:4; 3:10; 1:4

While time yet is, we may choose decisively, once and for all, to turn and face the front.

—⁓—

4

HIDE!

In Elijah's own country of Gilead, God cared for him, providing all his needs. He went to the brook named Cherith, the name of which signifies "cut off." So God cut off Elijah from all except His own faithful promise and provision. God had already commanded the ravens to feed him, caused the brook to flow with water, and cut off the supply of rain in the land.

God did not tell Elijah to prepare a backup plan and do everything he possibly could for himself. He simply directed him to hide in God and stay in God. Yes, his physical body was to hide at the brook, but his actual hiding place was in God.

One must make the choice to hide in God. Whether a prophet, a king, a widow, or a child, everyone needs a hiding place. In Psalm 32, God has explained His provision for our needs. We need:

1. A place where we can find forgiveness of
    sin and guilt: Life is full of temptations
    and pressures.

    Blessed is he whose transgression is forgiven,
    whose sin is covered.
    Blessed is the man unto whom
    the LORD imputeth not iniquity,
    and in whose spirit there is no guile.
    When I kept silence, my bones waxed old through
    my roaring all the day long.
    For day and night thy hand was heavy upon me:
    my moisture is turned into the drought of summer.
    . . .I acknowledged my sin unto thee,
    and mine iniquity have I not hid.
    I said, I will confess my transgressions unto the LORD;
    and thou forgavest the iniquity of my sin.
    PSALM 32:1–5

2. A place of companionship and joy: Life is
    lonely.

    For this shall every one that is godly
    pray unto thee in a time when
    thou mayest be found. . . .
    PSALM 32:6

3. A place of hope for the future: Life is full of uncertainty.

> *Thou art my hiding place;*
> *thou shalt preserve me from trouble;*
> *thou shalt compass me about*
> *with songs of deliverance.*
> PSALM 32:7

4. A place to receive instruction for living: Life is confusing.

> *I will instruct thee and teach thee*
> *in the way which thou shalt go.*
> PSALM 32:8

Elijah found that place: His hiding place was God. Jesus Christ is the same yesterday, today, and forever. He says:

> *Come unto me,*
> *all ye that labour and are heavy laden,*
> *and I will give you rest.*
> *Take my yoke upon you, and learn of me;*
> *. . .and ye shall find rest unto your souls.*
> MATTHEW 11:28–29

I have a place to hide!

Thy Hidden Ones

O Lord, Thine own are weary,
The streams of earth are dry,
The windy tempest hard doth flail,
Our longing spirits cry.

When will we hear that trumpet call,
Be safe fore'er with All-in-all?

Yet, LORD, Thou art our secret place,
Our shelter in the blast:
Thy shield immovable and sure
Throughout this life shall last.

Then we will hide with Christ in Thee
'Til all our troubles cease to be.

Then hearts rejoice, with wonder dumb:
Thy hidden ones what squall can numb?

It looks like it was Elijah, Elijah, and Elijah only hiding there by that brook. Elijah was all alone there, except for ravens twice a day. Ravens are scavenger birds from which most of us would instinctively cringe and run, but to Elijah they were the messengers of God's hand. It must have been a time of loneliness for Elijah there at the brook.

I can be lonely in a crowd
Or I can be alone and not be lonely;
It all depends, not on my surroundings,
But whether I am content with Jesus only.

When we are all alone, time seems to move very slowly; we become restless, worried, fearful, morbid, and depressed. But God has purpose for our quiet, alone times, as well as in the bustle of life. When we are alone, we can seek God with no distractions or time pressures, no interruptions, no telephone or doorbell, no duties calling. Try always to remember: Since God is there, too, we are never all alone!

Alone?

Dear Lord, I am all alone, but all alone with You.
If I'm with You and You're with me,
I am not alone and never could be!

—⁘—

5

GOD'S RAVENS

1 KINGS 17:6

And the ravens brought him
bread and flesh in the morning,
and bread and flesh in the evening.
1 KINGS 17:6

Where did the ravens get food to bring? Ravens are always regarded as omens of trouble, and according to Hebrew tradition, they are unclean. From somewhere, God provided the ravens with chunks of bread and meat to bring to Elijah. He never failed to have a meal every morning and evening. In Scripture there is nothing to indicate that he was anything but healthy during his campout at the brook.

It is good to look back and remember the way that God has filled my need. Maybe I cannot even recall all the little helps He put together to make it enough, but it was! How abundant is God's provision! He will never allow His children to lack any good thing. Always, all I have needed, God's hand has provided.

God shields from the scorching of the sun yet provides sunlight and warmth. Just so, I need the visible blessings of daily provision that God supplies without fail. I also need to be shielded from focusing on my selfish desires and from greedily clinging to the gifts God supplies as temporary provisions for this temporal life. God not only bestows with a lavish hand but also shields me from myself. When everything else is shadowed by my Shield, I look into the sunlight of His face, and all is well.

For the LORD God is a sun and shield:
the LORD will give grace and glory:
no good thing will he withhold
from them that walk uprightly.
PSALM 84:11

God so delights to bless His own! He says He withholds nothing at all that is good for us. All, yes, *all* I have needed, He has supplied. All I will need He will continue to supply in His perfect time —just the moment that I need it! How blessed is the one who trusts in Him!

God truly does use His servants from time to time to supply needs. It might be said that God has His "ravens" among us, folk who are sensitive to His voice bidding them to go and give. They unquestioningly heed God's word and obey it!

These people have given God their hearts and their possessions. They will probably never know until they reach God's presence how great the blessings were to those who received their gifts—how precious God's provision, through their hands, was to the one in need at that time! Nor will they understand all the thankfulness and rejoicing in God that their obedience brought.

But God rewards His faithful children. He is not unrighteous to forget a labor carried out because someone loves Him and is willing to be a raven for Him.

Whether ravens are sent to us at God's Brookside Hotel, where we are in need of daily provisions as Elijah was, or God sends us as a raven to someone who needs companionship, a hot meal, a hug, or a huge smile, we must trust in Him and obey Him. We will be fully satisfied, for we will feast on His faithfulness all the days of our lives.

There we are where God has sent us, doing what God has directed us to do, and we feel quite satisfied, for all is going well, until suddenly our world is turned upside down and maybe even inside out! The outward cause could be a lack of supply, a sorrow, a feeling of pressure to change our course, discontent with what has perfectly contented us until now, or simply inward restlessness. Maybe we fear change. We are in a comfortable rut, and it seems that God always provides for us in the same way. But God is not bound by any one method or source. When He says, "No more of this," He is signifying only that He has "much more" for us from another source.

Elijah had gone to the brook and hidden himself there. He had every necessary provision, and all was going well. Did he think he would live there and eat of Raven Room Service throughout the drought? Perhaps he did: It was working! It worked for about one year.

Then the brook dried up. God used natural events to show Elijah His will: The brook dried up because there was no rain. God could have kept it flowing if He so chose. Consternation, confusion, and uncontrollable fear could have overwhelmed Elijah. His physical source of sustenance ended when the brook dried up. It was to be expected, according to God's laws of nature, that the brook would dry up, but where was peace for Elijah when his very source of physical life vanished? God said, "Go and see!"

I do not need to be fearful when my regular means of provision cease. God is not saying I have been out of His will; He is showing me that His will includes changes, new directives, and new means of provision.

6

ALL DRIED UP

We have all heard of a well, a tiny stream, or a pond drying up, but think of an entire country drying up! It did not rain once in three and one-half years. No refreshing morning dew fell on the dusty, crusty soil or on anything else in the entire country. Without rain, even the waters of rivers and streams gradually evaporated and disappeared. The water supply in the wells was probably being strictly rationed, yet it became less and less each day, as even the ground itself became parched and cracked. Dusty, crusty, powdery. Bone dry. Samaria was all dried up, and the sun continued to sear the already-parched land.

The hair and lips, feet and hands of the people of the land became dry, rough, and cracked. How could they launder clothing or bedding, let alone

37

bathe their dehydrating bodies, when even drinking water was so scarce? How miserable—all dried up!

When God gave His message of the coming drought through Elijah, it said only, "there shall not be dew nor rain these years, but according to my word" (1 Kings 17:1). How many years? How long will it last? How long can we go on like this? The answer was, "as long as the LORD God in His sovereignty has planned"—not a second longer or a minute less.

Oh, King Ahab, when will you turn to the LORD? Oh, inhabitants of Samaria, when will you seek the LORD?

Sow to yourselves in righteousness, reap in mercy;
break up your fallow ground:
for it is time to seek the LORD,
till he come and rain righteousness upon you.
HOSEA 10:12

Will I let my heart become calloused and hard until God sends drought to our hearts? Will He have to cause us to be arid, fruitless, seared of joy? Or will we seek the Lord now?

When thou saidest, Seek ye my face;
my heart said unto thee,
Thy face, LORD, will I seek.
PSALM 27:8

Ye shall seek me, and find me,
when ye shall search for me with all your heart.
JEREMIAH 29:13

The LORD is good. . .
to the soul that seeketh him.
LAMENTATIONS 3:25

At a time of major change in my life, I struggle inwardly, my mind awash in the overwhelming waves of the unknown. *How do I. . .I wonder if I need to think of. . .? Can I make it? Seems like I can right now, but by end of the year, what will happen?*

I think I should do. . .but I wish. . .would happen, and I wish I did not have to think of. . . How do I plan, prepare? Yet, I do have everything I actually need *right this minute!*

When God provides bread and flesh in the morning and evening, my part is to eat it without question, doubt, or fear for lack of a meal tomorrow.

For I know the thoughts that I think toward you,
says the LORD, thoughts of peace and not of evil,
to give you a future and a hope.
JEREMIAH 29:11 NKJV

When Elijah stood before King Ahab, he expressed the certainty that the LORD God lives. It is evident that Elijah still believed that, and again he stepped out in faith to comply with God's directions. Since one cannot live without water, the dried-up brook had to mean God was leading him elsewhere.

And the word of the LORD came unto him, saying,
Arise, get thee to Zarephath. . .
behold, I have commanded a widow woman
there to sustain thee.
1 KINGS 17:8–9

As soon as a time of change arrived, God's instruction and means of continued provision were conveyed to Elijah.

God's word was there to comfort and guide Elijah throughout these challenges of change of residence and means of support. God stooped to Elijah's humanity and told him how he would be given food in the coming days, though Elijah would have to boldly cry out for that food to a destitute widow with a dependent child. Perhaps God sent Elijah to the helpless widow so he would realize afresh that his reliance and expectancy must be focused on God Himself, not only on the gifts God gives.

Elijah did not need to be afraid. God's Word explains,

But whoso hearkeneth unto me shall dwell safely,
and shall be quiet from fear of evil.
PROVERBS 1:33

What do I need today that my Father will not or cannot provide? The answer to that question is, "Nothing!" When He planned my life, God included within His eternal purpose the supply of my every need.

One must have water; yet the brook dried up. Elijah was helpless to stop the water from disappearing. It simply evaporated into the dry air. In the same way, I am helpless to provide my own needs today. *I am cast upon You, oh, Lord. By grace I will not fear, because You already know all about my need. You have planned to supply my need when I definitely need it.*

There is the key: When do I need it? If I insist on being prepared well ahead of the deadline, I may indeed feel fear, because I do not know where the provision is. But if I do not actually need it *right now,* right this minute, then I certainly cannot accuse God of not providing my need.

It is so easy to confuse wants with actual immediate needs. Separating the two helps. God tells us in Psalm 136:25 that He gives food to all flesh. I need to recognize that "gives" is in the present tense. He constantly gives all I need right now.

There have been times when I felt I had nothing at all. Yet there was never a time when I did not have something to eat at mealtime. Morning or evening, early or late (according to my personal calendar), God always provided in time. His promise to His own is that His people will never be ashamed.

Often He gives far more than my basic need. He gives more because He loves me, because He wants to give to me.

What will I do right now—right when I have a need?

I will wait on my God, Who is never neglectful, never late, never stingy. I will rejoice in Him alone, even as I enjoy the bounty of gifts He has provided, both material and spiritual. I will praise His name for His faithfulness and truth, and I will ever know and expect that all I need is my own.

If always I want
Only what I need,
Then always I have
All I want indeed.
For God has promised—
And He never will mislead:
But my God shall supply
All your need!

A brook will not dry up before breakfast is ready somewhere else.

Then, what want I more,
When now is mine
All, all of Christ
My Lord divine?

And the word of the LORD came unto him, saying, Arise, get thee to Zarephath, which belongeth to Zidon, and dwell there: behold, I have commanded a widow woman there to sustain thee. So he arose and went to Zarephath. And when he came to the gate of the city, behold, the widow woman was there gathering of sticks: and he called to her, and said, Fetch me, I pray thee, a little water in a vessel, that I may drink. And as she was going to fetch it, he called to her, and said, Bring me, I pray thee, a morsel of bread in thine hand. And she said, As the LORD thy God liveth, I have not a cake, but an handful of meal in a barrel, and a little oil in a cruse: and, behold, I am gathering two sticks, that I may go in and dress it for me and my son, that we may eat it, and die. And Elijah said unto her, Fear not; go and do as thou hast said: but make me thereof a little cake first, and bring it unto me, and after make for thee and for thy son. For thus saith the LORD God of Israel, The barrel of meal shall not waste, neither shall the cruse of oil fail, until the day that the LORD sendeth rain upon the earth. And she went and did according to the saying of Elijah: and she, and he, and her house, did eat many days. And the barrel of meal wasted not, neither did the cruse of oil fail, according to the word of the LORD, which he spake by Elijah.

1 KINGS 17:8–16

7

JUST GO

1 KINGS 17:10

God has promised that His own will hear a word saying, "This is the way, walk ye in it." He promises to guide His own continually and to satisfy. He warns us not to be as the mule. There is no need to be, for one trusting the Lord is compassed about with mercy.

> He that appointeth what the voyage
> shall be,
> will victual the ship accordingly.
> MATTHEW HENRY

Elijah had come this far by following God's word. The word of the true, living God had never yet failed him, and so he went to a destitute widow in Zarephath, and he candidly spoke all the words

God put into his mouth.

God was faithful, as He always is. The widow, her son, and Elijah ate for as long as the famine continued.

Elijah went. Elijah did. Elijah saw.

They that go. . .that do. . .
These see the works of the LORD,
and his wonders.
PSALM 107:23–24

Just go when God gives the directive!
Just get up and obey His wise word!
Each moment all needed He will
    fully supply,
And the reason you may learn in the
    sweet by and by.

If, after awhile, I hear a word from the Lord, I, too, will get up and go where He leads me, do what He directs me to do. Then I will surely come again with rejoicing. Constantly, I am realizing God's wonderful provision for my every need and the desires of my heart, as I do His will. Perhaps, by being obedient, I will be used to encourage others in yielding to Him, too.

I may at first think that this new way cannot possibly work. When I get set in my old way, my own way, that seems to be the only viable option. But God's ways are higher; His thoughts are far above my human wisdom. No matter what the circumstance or how difficult the way looks, God's commanding word comes to me with a certain cruse of oil, ceaselessly full to capacity for my consumption and dissemination.

So Elijah arose and went.

Heed His Word

The billowing clouds gracefully sweep
To form the dust about God's feet.
From His treasuries His wind He brings,
And through the boughs and leaves it sings.
Snow like wool He sendeth from heaven;
His ice like morsels in torrents are given;
By His breath cometh frost in delicate flakes,
Intricate, perfect patterns to make;
And then, with only His word, "Go!"
All dissolveth of ice and snow.
The birds take flight from clime to clime,

Following only their Maker's time;
He giveth the instinct to every beast,
From lion great to mousie least,
To naturally follow God's perfect plan,
And He feedeth them from His own hand.
God knoweth surely what He is about;
Can I by searching find Him out?
Could I do less than to heed His word,
Whenever or wherever it is heard?
No, I shall straightly get up and go,
Obey like the birds, the wind, and the snow.

8

THERE

1 KINGS 17:8–10

Again the word of the LORD came.
God always has a *there* for me, a place where He has determined I ought to be. He has made provision for my sustenance there in that place. When God sent me to the foreign mission field, I did not need to fear going, for I knew that God was already there. In His sovereignty, He had commanded some of His servants at home to provide for my sustenance while I was serving Him there. God not only plans and provides for foreign missionaries; He guides and provides for each of His children in the place of His choosing.

Elijah's *there*, the place where God told him to go, was Zarephath. The name signifies a melting pot or refinement. This, then, was the place God was going to further shape His vessel of clay, to smooth some rough edges that would keep him from being all that God desired him to be and from doing everything that God had planned for him to do. Only in God's melting pot can a life be refined and made suitable for God's service.

As was his practice, Elijah obeyed God's word. When he went, he found provision for his needs, for God's practice is to keep His word. The widow woman was there. The necessary grain and oil were there. The widow could not yet see the ephahs of grain or the hins of oil, but a promise from God is a fact! God had promised that Elijah would be fed there. Obviously this would also include sustenance for the one feeding him.

Elijah arose and went to Zarephath. God was already there, of course, and had brought the widow there to the gate of the city. Elijah did not have to wonder which way to go or where to look—there she was!

Some nine hundred years before Elijah's time, the servant of Abraham was sent on a lengthy journey back to Abraham's kindred to choose a wife for Abraham's son, Isaac. The servant went where he was commanded and found there Rebekah, the perfect bride for his master's son. His testimony was:

I being in the way, the LORD led me. . . .
GENESIS 24:27

He went in the way God directed him to go, the way that led directly to God's provision. There was the bride to be. God had prepared her heart also, so she was ready and willing to go with the servant and become Isaac's wife.

God told Elijah to go and live there. He went. God's plan included someone already there to provide for his sustenance. Elijah, too, was in God's way—the way God led.

Wherever God sends me, whatever He tells me to do, He has already commanded my sustenance there. God does not send me where I can make my own way, where I can see ahead, or where I can be in control. He places me where I must wait on His way, where I must trust moment by moment, where I must allow my times to rest in His hand.

Right there, where God has sent me, is the place where I know I need not fear nor worry. I know it is so, because I will be there with my God.

I'm Fine Today, Lord
(But what happens tomorrow?)

I said, "Father, this is hard—not knowing
From whence what I need shall come."
But He gently asked, "Why is it hard
When you know that I'm the One
Who is the Father and Provider,
Who has promised you shall not lack,
Who has every bit you need in store,
And will never a necessity hold back?"

So when no means on earth I can
    search out,
Still God knows exactly what He is about!
He is not perplexed concerning how or
    when.
Eternally He has each blessing in His hand.
Then I will trust when I cannot see
What way my God will provide for me.
I'll be glad when He to me the means
    confides;
But 'til then, by faith I expect Him to
    provide.

9

ONLY A HANDFUL

1 KINGS 17:10–11

God said to Elijah, "See, I have commanded a widow there to provide for you."

I have walked through city streets and byways in Bangladesh and India, and I could not escape seeing destitute beggars. Some were no more than scantily clad skin-and-bones bodies; some little children owned no clothing. Sunken, pleading eyes confirmed the desperate need, and palms were extended expectantly. If I could safely give to them without being mobbed, I delighted to do so. But never, never did I ask one of them to give me a piece of bread or even a drink of water. I wonder if Elijah felt some reticence when it came to asking the poor widow woman for help.

This woman did not have even one decent meal ahead for herself and son. She had only one fistful of meal to make a little cake. There were many widows in the area, Dr. Luke informs us (Luke 4:25–26), but God sent Elijah to this particular widow. Did He not know her destitution? Certainly. His plan included feeding her and her son, as well as Elijah.

God's plan also included bringing the widow to know God in a deeper way, more personally, confidingly. Elijah probably was unaware of the far-reaching miracles God was to effect during his stay in her home. Those miracles were to be set in motion by his asking for the bare necessities from one who had none to give.

Elijah did what God told him to do: He asked. He received food for his hungry stomach and a place to stay during the rest of the famine. He also let God use him as an instrument to aid in fulfilling God's plan for the widow's growth and blessing.

What if Elijah had refused to ask? What if he had insisted that she was too poor? What if he had given in to a wave of shyness? What if he had been ready to hold out for a full meat-and-potatoes and apple-pie dinner, rather than the basic water and barley cake God had chosen for him? How could a stranger walk up to one already destitute and ask for a meal? There was only a bite for the ones living in the home that day, and there was no handy convenience store on any corner in the whole land.

In Genesis 19:16–19 the angels led Lot away from the wicked city of Sodom because God was going to destroy the city. They told Lot to leave the flatland and escape to the mountain. But Lot replied, "Oh, not so, my Lord: Behold now, thy servant hath found grace in thy sight, and thou hast magnified thy mercy, which thou hast shewed unto me in saving my life; and I cannot escape to the mountain, lest some evil take me, and I die." Then he proceeded to offer his own suggestion as to a city where he desired to go. Sadly, Lot seemed to think he had more wisdom than the LORD God.

Elijah did not refuse when God spoke to him. He did not offer his own suggestions. He may not have liked to ask of the widow, but he followed God's directive nonetheless.

The entire event came about in God's way, God's time, through God's direction. God was in control of the outcome: Elijah could ask without fear. And God was going to provide a miracle! He would make the widow's one handful of grain into months of family meals, sufficient to satisfy hunger and maintain the health of each member of the household.

Shall not the Judge of all the earth do right?
GENESIS 18:25

Will I Lack?

When I have not resources
at my hand,
I cannot see how needs
will be met.
When I feel pressed against
that near deadline
And my faith
seems to be all but spent,

Underneath are the hands
of the Master
And His arms strong
to carry me through.
And mine are His
infinite treasures
Of all time
and eternity, too!

Could I lack since He
is my Shepherd?
Should I fear when my Lord
is "I AM"?
Or shall I seek my own way
to shoulder,
When He says to receive
from His hand?

No, I'll lean on those arms
all sufficient;
I'll accept my supply
from His store.
And no want shall I know
now or ever,
For He always has
abundantly more!

10

PREACH WHAT YOU PRACTICE!

1 KINGS 17:15–16

Elijah must have made a convincing request of the widow. I suppose it was not hard to do so, since he would have no dinner if he did not ask for it or she did not respond positively to the request.

Elijah had already experienced what he was asking the widow to do. He was preaching what he already practiced. He had acted on God's command to go to the brook Cherith and stay there. God had said the ravens would feed him: They did. Elijah had experience under his belt.

With no hesitation, Elijah encouraged the widow to act in faith, as he had done. He spoke God's word confidently and explicitly: Bring me a little cake first, and after make some for you and your son. Note that word *after* in verse 13! With this word, he was assuring her that God was indeed going to supply all her need: There would be meal and oil left for her after she fed him.

Elijah asked the woman to step out in faith, to give the last she had. He was preaching what he had practiced and had found to be infallible: God's word.

A child does as his parent directs. A wife follows as her husband leads. The parent and the husband are well-known to the one they instruct. They have proven themselves believable, reliable. So the instructed one obeys.

This widow probably did not know Elijah. One day he walked up and humbly but confidently asked her to do something that sounded foolish and impossible. Was it not foolish to give her family's last bit of food to a stranger? Was it not impossible that what she possessed could provide more than one scanty meal? Yet she complied.

Does God expect us to give what we need for sustenance? He asked the widow to give her bread to Elijah when she only had enough to feed herself and her son one more meal. God was asking for the last bite she had to feed her child. How could a mother say yes to such a request? She could obey only by the grace of God, Who was directing her to do so.

God spoke through Elijah, promising He

would see to it that there would be enough food for as long as He withheld the rain. She gave the only handful she had to God, and He blessed her faithfully, according to His promise. He supplied meal and oil every day for her and her family and Elijah through all the days of the drought, which continued more than two years. When God's word guarantees all needs will be provided, He means *all!*

She may have used up all the ground barley and oil each time she prepared a meal, yet she never had to wonder what they would eat for the next repast. When tomorrow's dinnertime came, God's provision of meal was there in her flour bin and oil cruse.

So when I have just enough for what I need today, I have all I need! If tomorrow comes, my faithful God, the LORD God, will supply all I need tomorrow.

Should I always expect that God wants me to give away what I truly need? Only if He specifically tells me so, and that will only happen when He plans to meet my need in His own wonderful way. Sometimes He asks beyond physical or emotional power, sometimes beyond pocketbook, often beyond my puny credence. Do I trust God completely? If so, I can say, "Yes, Lord." I can step out onto nothing and find my feet firmly planted on the Rock.

Go thy way;
and as thou hast believed,
so be it done unto thee.
MATTHEW 8:13

The widow discounted all impossibilities and followed God's word. That is true faith!

And she, and he,
and her house,
did eat many days.
1 KINGS 17:15

No specific number of days is given here, but God wrote this encouragement for believers today, as well as for that widow, who lived about 900 B.C.

Those paper towels that drop one at a time out of a dispenser seem so small. I have often grasped the towel and tried to pull the next one down along with it. Of course, this only causes frustration and waste, because the machine pauses a prescribed number of seconds before releasing the next towel. I have learned that if I accept the first towel available, tearing it off, then, presto, the next rolls down neatly and nicely and available to finish drying my hands.

So it was with that final scanty bit of grain and oil. The widow was willing and used it to serve her heaven-sent guest; God replaced the meal in her barrel and the oil in her jug. I wonder if she ever went and looked right before bedtime or right after breakfast and found it empty, just as she had left it? She did not need it then, but God had said it "would not waste." So it must have been that when she lifted out the last handful, God at the same time replenished the handful in the barrel. Thus it would never have wasted, that is, never was used up, for about two years. This—as everything —is possible with God. And true!

It appears the widow took up the challenge of Elijah's implicit trust in God and exercised the same faith. She must have wondered, *Who says so?* It was not only Elijah asking for food; it was God using Elijah to stir the woman into acting upon what she professed to believe. In the months to come, God was going to lead her into and on through much greater tests of faith than giving up one dinner.

God does that—tests one's faith! But He promised:

God is faithful
[to His Word and to His compassionate nature],
and He [can be trusted]
not to let you be tempted and tried. . .
beyond your ability and strength. . .

to endure, but. . .
He will [always] also provide. . .
the means. . .that you may be capable. . .
patiently to bear up under it.
1 Corinthians 10:13 Amplified

She had enough to feed them all for as many days as the drought lasted, as many days as her need lasted. God counts out the perfect number of days in His perfect wisdom, but He may provide just one moment—even just one meal—at a time.

Great is thy faith:
be it unto thee even as thou wilt.
Matthew 15:28

Possible!

A coin found in a fish's mouth,
Fresh water from out of a rock—
My God will provide every need
Whether it's possible or not!
A widow fed the prophet Elijah
The very last meal of her store:
Yet every day for months to come
From the emptiness she took out more!
"Can't" is only an earth-life word,
And as humans, some things we cannot,
But the Master of the universe can—
Whether it's possible or not!

I can follow God's directives and eat all I need from the cruse of oil of His Holy Spirit and the bin of the Bread of Life. Or I can choose to find my own way. But why? Why settle for the corn husks of this world, when in Christ my Lord I am guaranteed all I need? Never! Never! Never will He fail to provide all I need.

The LORD is my shepherd;
I shall not want. . . .
Surely goodness and mercy shall follow me
all the days of my life.
PSALM 23:1, 6

11

Peace, and at Such a Time!

1 Kings 16:29–17:16

God placed Elijah in a situation where he could not make his own way. He had no cellar, not even a knapsack. God wanted Elijah's entire expectancy to be in God. He was going to show Elijah the truth and reliability of His infallible word, so Elijah had no provision other than the water of the brook and what God sent by Raven Delivery twice daily.

My God has cast me on Himself,
But what other place to be,
Than resting on the heart of Him
Who died and lives for me!

In this entire account of Elijah's speaking to

King Ahab, dwelling at the brook, and then being used by God again in Zarephath, there is nothing to indicate that Elijah's mind-set was anything other than peacefully trusting His God. He had peace during the solitary time at the brook. He demonstrated peaceful assurance when he spoke to the widow and promised nonexistent food. Imagine—peace, and at such a time!

Thou wilt keep him in perfect peace,
whose mind is stayed on thee:
because he trusteth in thee.
ISAIAH 26:3

It is God Who is doing the keeping, because He is the Almighty, the nourisher, sustainer, satisfier. The one kept by Him may rest safely, contentedly in His keeping. God is able to keep heart and mind in perfect peace. That peace is complete in all respects, without defect or omission. Elijah allowed God to be the keeper. To be aware of God's will denotes a mind stayed or focused upon God, a heart open to receive the peace offered to His own. It is a peace no one can ever fabricate. God alone gives this true peace as a gift. It is never obtained by trying, but by trusting. It is provided to the one who rests on God's wisdom and strength.

Trust ye in the LORD for ever:
for in the LORD Jehovah is everlasting strength.
ISAIAH 26:4

Elijah lived in the peaceful pastures of God's will through aloneness, change, destitution, long periods of sitting still and waiting. Through God's word, we can sense Elijah's inward peace and see its outward expression in 1 Kings 17:1–16. The peace is revealed in:

- Elijah's acting on the *certainty* of his heart that the LORD God lives and is the true God of Israel—and of Elijah (v. 1).
- *Confidence* of his speech to King Ahab (v. 1).
- Elijah's *communion* with his God (vv. 2–4).
- God's *command* directly from His heart to Elijah's heart (v. 2).
- Elijah's *compliance* with God's directives (v. 5).
- *Comestibles.* God provided to satisfy physical hunger (v. 6).
- Elijah's rising to the *challenge* of facing new circumstances (vv. 5–6).
- Elijah's receiving *confirmation* of God's directive word. God is reliable (v. 6).
- Elijah's *continuing* to listen for God's guidance and accepting a *contract* providing for

the coming days (vv. 8–9).

- *Compliance* once again with God's will (v. 10).
- *Cognizance:* Indeed, the widow woman was there! Step by step God was fulfilling His word to Elijah (v. 10).
- Elijah's *calling* to the widow, asking for what God had promised (v. 10).
- A *cruse* of oil—a positive beginning for a dinner. In Scripture, oil was used in sacrifices, indicating joy or gladness. If there was no oil, sorrow or humiliation was indicated. God was not going to humiliate His servant by allowing any promise to fail (v. 12).
- *Candidly* Elijah spoke what God put into his mind, heart, and mouth (vv. 13–14).
- *Confirmation,* outward and visible, that Elijah had heard God's word and had spoken according to God's will. God performed what He had promised! (vv. 15–16).

Elijah is an imitable example of one who knew his God so well that he also knew perfect peace— and at such a time!

PART 2

"BY THIS I KNOW"

1 KINGS 17:17–18:46; JAMES 5:17

INTRODUCTION

Elijah, in obedience to God's word, had spoken to a king, stayed alone by a brook, sought food from a destitute widow, and seen God's miraculous provision through it all. But Elijah's stay at Zarephath was not yet complete. God had another test, probably the greatest proving of Elijah's and the widow's faith. Then the LORD would send His word a third time, instructing Elijah where to go next, what to do when he got there, and what to say. Elijah was to be used by God to bring about a miracle that would affect the entire nation, from the king to the menials.

Oh, Mr. Elijah, remain ever faithful to your God!

—⚬—

12

WHAT FELLOWSHIP IS THIS?

JAMES 5:17

"Subject to like passions as we are" is what James offers as a description of Elijah of the Old Testament. Elijah experienced the same feelings and affections we experience. It is safe to deduce that he feared, hesitated, doubted, and dreaded. He walked on with God and learned to appropriate God's presence and peace, power and persistence. He also claimed God's answers to his prayers uttered by the word of heart desire.

When it comes to the prayer of faith, we must look up and ask God for delight in Him that will not entertain doubt. Such faith only comes through knowing God personally, seeking His heart, receiving from Him the burden for specific requests, and depending totally upon Him. As He enables, we can boldly pray in Jesus' name. Faith will not fail to receive, for it is God Himself Who promised to answer such prayer.

The Scripture says Elijah prayed in earnestness. He was fervent and persevered in prayer. He did not suddenly find himself in need, look up, and say: *God, I am Elijah, and am I glad to meet You, because I hear that You will dole out whatever I need right now.*

> *Elias was a man subject to*
> *like passions as we are,*
> *and he prayed earnestly that it might not rain:*
> *and it rained not on the earth*
> *by the space of three years and six months.*
> JAMES 5:17

Elijah obviously had come to catch the ear of God! The eternal God was Elijah's God. Elijah had believed on Him. Then must have followed learning from God daily, growing through keeping company with God. Though he was a man of like passions with us, Elijah asked and received from the God of heaven and earth! When we are at one with a friend, fellowship is sweet, and there is nothing best friends would not do for each other.

Such salvation God has offered to mortals! He created me, formed every part of my being for Himself. He gave life and breath to the body and soul that I claim as myself. But I was conceived of human parents, who had the sin nature, born as a human being with that same sin nature. This nature began with our first parents in the Garden of Eden. Thus I had to realize my sinful condition and receive the gift of God—eternal life. It is provided free to everyone who believes, for Jesus paid the wages of sin on the cross of Calvary.

Elijah evidently walked in submission to God and in personal camaraderie with God. Elijah could go to his friend, God, anytime. What a blessing is a friend to whom one can go—early or late, in dire distress or for pleasant sharing—and find a ready reception!

Elijah communed with his God according to his need, and God responded with miracles indeed! This had to be the result of his taking time to become a friend of God and a friend to God.

What fellowship is this,
that the God of all creation
Should stoop to hear my heart's desire
and respond with affirmation?

God says, "The prayer of faith shall save the sick, and the Lord shall raise him up" (James 5:15). Elijah was about to put this principle to the test.

—∿—

And it came to pass after these things, that the son of the woman, the mistress of the house, fell sick; and his sickness was so sore, that there was no breath left in him. And she said unto Elijah, What have I to do with thee, O thou man of God? art thou come unto me to call my sin to remembrance, and to slay my son? And he said unto her, Give me thy son. And he took him out of her bosom, and carried him up into a loft, where he abode, and laid him upon his own bed. And he cried unto the L<small>ORD</small>, and said, O L<small>ORD</small> my God, hast thou also brought evil upon the widow with whom I sojourn, by slaying her son? And he stretched himself upon the child three times, and cried unto the L<small>ORD</small>, and said, O L<small>ORD</small> my God, I pray thee, let this child's soul come into him again. And the L<small>ORD</small> heard the voice of Elijah; and the soul of the child came into him again, and he revived. And Elijah took the child, and brought him down out of the chamber into the house, and delivered him unto his mother: and Elijah said, See, thy son liveth. And the woman said to Elijah, Now by this I know that thou art a man of God, and that the word of the L<small>ORD</small> in thy mouth is truth.

1 K<small>INGS</small> 17:17–24

13

GOD'S WORD IS TRUTH

1 KINGS 17:24

In a traumatic hour, we may not think clearly, may frantically search for reasons why, and may look for someone or something to blame.

> *Thy words have upholden him that was falling,*
> *and thou hast strengthened the feeble knees.*
> *But now it is come upon thee,*
> *and thou faintest;*
> *it toucheth thee, and thou art troubled.*
> JOB 4:4–5

When her son died, the widow cried to Elijah, asking, "Did you come to call my sin to remembrance and to kill my son?" But when a loved one dies, it is not because of our wrongdoing. The day and moment of death are a part of God's plan for every individual He has created. We may with great joy take comfort in the truth that resurrection is also in that plan.

My times are in thy hand. . .
Oh, how great is thy goodness,
which thou hast laid up for them that fear thee;
which thou hast wrought for them
that trust in thee before the sons of men!
PSALM 31:15, 19

Shouldn't the widow logically expect, after all she had done for God's prophet, that God would care for everything that concerned her? But her son died. As far as we are told, he was her only son. Certainly she was troubled and probably frantic. In her misery and confusion, she asked Elijah what she had done against him. But death was not in Elijah's power, nor was life. God was going to provide an amazing visual example of His truth and power.

Elijah did not argue with her, but authoritatively spoke: "Give me thy son." She needed direction at these initial moments of comprehending her loss. She complied, allowing Elijah to take the lad from her arms. He took the lifeless form; he shifted the burden from her heart to his own, and carried it up to his loft chamber.

He placed the body of the son upon his bed

and then what else could he do but cry out to God? Elijah did not understand why God had done this. He cried out with all helplessness, and probably in astonishment and wonder, asking whether God really desired to bring this calamity on the widow who had provided a home for him. God readily responded by giving Elijah faith strong enough to ask the humanly impossible. He prayed in faith, making a specific request that God would restore the child's life.

Elijah had the kind of faith that trusts what God promises and takes what God provides.

He prayed earnestly and with sincerity of faith. He walked heart-to-heart with God. Then God could reveal to Elijah's heart what He planned to do. At that point, Elijah cast all of himself on the credibility of eternal God. He placed himself between the dead body and the living God. He reposed on God. God rewarded that trust: "And the soul of the child came into him again, and he revived" (1 Kings 17:22).

Try to imagine the amazement, the astonishment Elijah knew at that moment!

"I am always amazed at God's goodness," my friend exclaimed one morning as we shared special blessings over the phone. I voiced amazement, too, but I wondered if we should be in awe when God simply does what He has promised to do. I have decided that I ought to fully expect His doing, but also should never lose sight of the wonder of His personal attention to each of His children.

Amazement encompasses various areas of thought and attitude.

- Wonder. I am excited because what is going on is great! God is working in me, for me, and through me, and in all creation.
- Admiration. Wonder includes delight and pleased approval. It offers pleasurable contemplation of God and His gifts.
- Awe. Reverential fear is not trembling terror but holy submission quivering with peace and joy. This is mine because I respect Who God is. I stand in awe of His majesty.
- Dumbfoundedness. I am speechless, feeling excitement, astonishment, and wondering awe overwhelming me.

Until we reach heaven, I agree with my friend: "Let me be amazed!"

Elijah must have experienced all of this and more. I feel a bit of it every time I read God's account of the resurrection of this lad. "And the LORD heard the voice of Elijah." Oh, the wonder of it all—eternal God.

Who only hath immortality,
dwelling in the light which no man can approach unto;
whom no man hath seen, nor can see. . .
1 TIMOTHY 6:16

This God listened to the voice of one man who was as mortal, sinful, and helpless as you and I! When God leads one to pray a specific request, He has planned to do that thing.

Remember Hannah? Hannah was barren and sorely desired a child. She went to the temple with her husband and prayed that God would remember her and give them a child. She believed in her heart that God had heard her prayer, and Eli the priest agreed with her. He said, "Go in peace: and the God of Israel grant thee thy petition that thou hast asked of him" (1 Samuel 1:17). Hannah went her way, ate, and smiled.

She had not yet conceived the child, yet she knew she had received the answer to her prayer, for she knew the LORD would keep His word. (And He did!)

It was the same with Elijah. God received Elijah's prayer and responded by restoring the child's life.

—⁓—

14

"BY THIS I KNOW"

1 KINGS 17:24

The widow, mother of the resurrected lad, made a strong, positive statement. "Now by this I know. . .that the word of the LORD. . .is truth." But how could she be sure? How did she reach this place of certainty?

First, she trusted all she had left on earth to God. She gave the body of her only son into Elijah's arms. Then she allowed Elijah to take her son away from her, out of her sight. She did not try to follow; she trusted her burden to the man of God. However, I expect she remained as close as possible to the ladder leading to Elijah's loft. There was no video camera in the loft conveying the happenings "live" to the first floor of the little home. All she had was faith in her God, so in faith she waited below.

Your mother, your child, your friend, your sibling, your spouse—each believing dear one gone on ahead—is in the arms of the heavenly Father. You do not know what it is like in heaven, or exactly what is going on up there. Yet you may choose to:

- trust the body, soul, and spirit of your dear one to those everlasting arms.
- cast your burden on the Lord. Let Him carry the burden and you.
- allow God to make the decisions.
- stay close to God when He allows heartache. "Though he slay me, yet will I trust in him" (Job 13:15).
- wait expectantly. Hope in God! "Abraham believed God. . .who quickeneth the dead. . . . And being not weak in faith. . .he staggered not at the promise of God through unbelief; but was strong in faith. . .and being fully persuaded that, what he had promised, he was able also to perform" (Romans 4:3, 17, 19–21).

A little boy comes with a drooping yellow dandelion clenched in a chubby fist. "See! It's for you, Mommy!" A cherubic girl child with golden curls offers a scribbled paper. "I made it just for you, Daddy! See!"

Though we have outgrown wilting wildflowers and colored scribbles, we still certainly enjoy coming to a friend to say, "See! This is what God has done!"

So Elijah took the restored child back down to the waiting mother and exclaimed, "See, thy son liveth." The mother's testimony was, "Now by this I know that thou art a man of God, and that the word of the LORD in thy mouth is truth" (1 Kings 17:24).

What will it be like when Jesus takes us to heaven and says, "See, here is your loved one, perfect, and whole, and like Me!" We will be reunited in fully satisfying, never-ending joy!

Then we will know with surety, without doubt, and forever that the Word of God is true! But we can trust God's word now, even in death. He has promised, "I am the resurrection, and the life: he that believeth in me, though he were dead, yet shall he live: and whosoever liveth and believeth in me shall never die" (John 11:25). Do you believe this?

The promise is certain for each individual—from the beginning of time until the end of it—who believes in the Lord Jesus Christ for forgiveness of sin. The house of clay, that vehicle God has provided us for living on earth, doing His will, and glorifying His name, may wear out and die. It will be left below for now. But soul and spirit will live—immediately at leaving the body and forever—in God's presence. Even the body will be resurrected and changed to fitness for life in eternity. First Corinthians 15 tells that it will be changed to be like Jesus' glorified body. Body, soul, and spirit will be reunited when Jesus comes in the Rapture to call all believers to be with Him eternally.

Elijah could never give life: God alone holds the breath of life.

He cried to the LORD and said,
O LORD my God,
have You brought further calamity
upon the widow with whom I sojourn,
by slaying her son?
1 KINGS 17:20 AMPLIFIED

This event with the widow's son in about 910 B.C. was the first recorded that God restored a human to life on earth. God usually does not do that. Instead, He Himself will fill the emptiness gaping in the heart of a loved one left behind. He Himself will be all that is needed to the sorrowing heart. We hurt with the pain of loss that defies description, but we do not understand everything that is going on up there in heaven. We may rest assured that our believing dear one is looking on the face of the Savior, the Son of God, the Bright and Morning Star, the Lord of our salvation, Immanuel—that is, "God with us."

He is with us! He is nearer than our very self. Our dear one is never very far from us, because we are together within the heart of our Father God.

The widow asked if Elijah had come to call her sin to remembrance because her son died. But when a loved one dies, it is not our fault. God is not punishing us because we did some wrong. Our times are in God's hand. The day and moment of physical death is part of God's plan for each of us. That is true until the moment Jesus returns in the clouds and calls each of His own still alive on earth home to be with Him forever.

We can continue victoriously here on earth because we know that the Word of God is truth, and by this Word we have assurance that, after awhile, we will be forever together.

And it came to pass after many days, that the word of the LORD came to Elijah in the third year, saying, Go, shew thyself unto Ahab; and I will send rain upon the earth. And Elijah went to shew himself unto Ahab. And there was a sore famine in Samaria. And Ahab called Obadiah, which was the governor of his house. (Now Obadiah feared the LORD greatly: for it was so, when Jezebel cut off the prophets of the LORD, that Obadiah took an hundred prophets, and hid them by fifty in a cave, and fed them with bread and water.) And Ahab said unto Obadiah, Go into the land, unto all fountains of water, and unto all brooks: peradventure we may find grass to save the horses and mules alive, that we lose not all the beasts. So they divided the land between them to pass throughout it: Ahab went one way by himself, and Obadiah went another way by himself. And as Obadiah was in the way, behold, Elijah met him: and he knew him, and fell on his face, and said, Art thou that my lord Elijah? And he answered him, I am: go, tell thy lord, Behold, Elijah is here. And he said, What have I sinned, that thou wouldest deliver thy servant into the hand of Ahab, to slay me? As the LORD thy God liveth, there is no nation or kingdom, whither my lord hath not sent to seek thee: and when they said, He is not there; he took an oath of the kingdom and nation, that they found thee not.

And now thou sayest, Go, tell thy lord, Behold, Elijah is here. And it shall come to pass, as soon as I am gone from thee, that the Spirit of the LORD shall carry thee whither I know not; and so when I come and tell Ahab, and he cannot find thee, he shall slay me: but I thy servant fear the LORD from my youth. Was it not told my lord what I did when Jezebel slew the prophets of the LORD, how I hid an hundred men of the LORD's prophets by fifty in a cave, and fed them with bread and water? And now thou sayest, Go, tell thy lord, Behold, Elijah is here: and he shall slay me. And Elijah said, As the LORD of hosts liveth, before whom I stand, I will surely shew myself unto him to day.

So Obadiah went to meet Ahab, and told him: and Ahab went to meet Elijah.

1 KINGS 18:1–16

15

GOD NEVER
FORGETS TO REMEMBER

1 KINGS 18:1

The days Elijah dwelt at Zarephath, after leaving the brook Cherith, added up to about two years and five months. What was he thinking? Had God forgotten him? He had only been at the brook for approximately one year when God had given him the next directive: "Arise, get thee to Zarephath. . . and dwell there" (1 Kings 17:9). The word *dwell* could mean "linger" or "make your home there," so perhaps Elijah was not sure that God would send him anywhere else. After about two and one-half years, one becomes quite settled in as a part of the community. But even before his coming into Samaria, The Amplified Bible refers to Elijah as "one of the temporary residents of Gilead." I guess Elijah was ever "on call," ready to serve God wherever and whenever.

Then there it was: God's instruction to Elijah to return to the palace in Samaria and let King Ahab know that Elijah was alive and well. God was also! And God was fulfilling His Word. He never forgets to remember. God let Elijah in on His plan to soon send rain.

Elijah stepped out to obey God, going to show himself to King Ahab. The king was in desperate straits as a result of the years of drought. The land had dried up; nothing was sprouting; nothing was left in the larders.

It doesn't appear that King Ahab had any inkling of how many years it would be before rain again satisfied the thirsty land. God's message through Elijah only said "these years" (1 Kings 17:1). Perhaps all that Elijah knew was that God was in control.

This time Elijah wasn't going off alone, where ravens were the only living beings he would encounter. Going there, he would not have "lost face" if the ravens had not brought food at God's command. (He might have died, though!)

This time he was to go and stand again before that wicked ruler who probably had been cursing Elijah for the past three years, blaming him for the impoverished condition of his entire kingdom.

"And Elijah went" (1 Kings 18:2). What volumes those words speak! Elijah knew what God desired, he knew God's trustworthiness, and he stepped out in obedience. Abraham did that, too.

By faith Abraham,
when he was called to go out. . .obeyed;
and he went out, not knowing whither he went.
HEBREWS 11:8

What is God directing you to do today? When He says, "Go, and I will provide all that you need today," may you never find yourself heavy with remorse because you did not believe God and act upon His Word.

God never fails to carry out His Word completely. When we have "the hope of the promise made of God" (Acts 26:6), we do not need to worry or fear. God will not forget to remember to do as He has spoken.

16

Nevertheless I Will

1 Kings 18:3–16

God required Elijah to witness to King Ahab. The king was desperate now: He could not find water—or Elijah.

The king and his steward were searching the entire countryside for any bits of grass to feed the horses and mules. What would they do if their livestock died? The king decided to go throughout the land to all the brooks, to see if perchance one yet contained water. He and his steward went in opposite directions. God sent Elijah to the area that Obadiah was searching.

"Yeah, sure you will," countered Obadiah to Elijah's promise that he would present himself to the king. "You say I should tell King Ahab you are here. But as sure as I get the words out of my mouth, God will whisk you away by His Spirit to a place I don't know. Then the king will kill me!

"You know, Elijah, King Ahab has scoured the entire country, and every other country around us, looking for you. He demanded that every nation swear they had not found you in their kingdom.

"If I go tell the king you are here and you disappear again, he will have my head! But I have feared God since I was young. Did you not hear that I hid one hundred of God's prophets in caves and fed them? I have been faithful to our God!"

Obadiah, whose name means "servant or worshiper of Yahweh," had faithfully served God, even while serving as King Ahab's steward. What an unlikely combination of duties! It is a curiosity that the king employed this believer. Yet, if one can serve a secular employer honestly and well and still not compromise his faith, he may bear faithful witness of the God he loves and serves. He may do so even without spoken testimony. Surely he will, as a servant of God, be loyal to his employer, honest in all his dealings, and a willing worker.

That we may lead a quiet and
peaceable life in all godliness and honesty.
For this is good and acceptable in
the sight of God our Saviour;
Who will have all men to be saved,
and to come unto the knowledge of the truth.
1 TIMOTHY 2:2–4

If we truly love, reverence, and trust God, we will continue to honor Him in bad or hard times, just as we do in the midst of good and pleasant times. Evidently Obadiah did so. Jezebel executed the prophets of God, probably to try to do away with Elijah, but Obadiah hid one hundred prophets of God in caves and faithfully provided bread and water for their sustenance.

Elijah promised Obadiah in God's name that he would surely present himself to Ahab that very day. So Obadiah carried the announcement back to his employer.

In the Gospel of Luke, it is related that Jesus told Peter to cast his net on the right side of the ship, and he would catch fish. Peter had reason not to obey, for he had been casting his net into the water repeatedly all night long and pulling it back in empty! But he concluded: "Nevertheless at thy word I will let down the net" (Luke 5:5).

So did Obadiah. Though he first complained and hesitated in fear, he yielded to God's will, returning to meet the king and delivering Elijah's message.

And it came to pass, when Ahab saw Elijah, that Ahab said unto him, Art thou he that troubleth Israel? And he answered, I have not troubled Israel; but thou, and thy father's house, in that ye have forsaken the commandments of the LORD, and thou hast followed Baalim. Now therefore send, and gather to me all Israel unto mount Carmel, and the prophets of Baal four hundred and fifty, and the prophets of the groves four hundred, which eat at Jezebel's table. So Ahab sent unto all the children of Israel, and gathered the prophets together unto mount Carmel.

1 KINGS 18:17–20

17

IT'S ALL YOUR FAULT

Elijah, of course, kept his word to Obadiah and made himself available when King Ahab came to meet him. The king asked Elijah, "Art thou he that troubleth Israel?"

King Ahab had led his entire kingdom of northern Israel into hideous idolatry. God, who bears long with human foolishness and frailties, was provoked to great anger. Now Ahab calls God's prophet the one who troubles Israel. But when one knowingly, willfully, and boldly chooses to disobey God and leads others into sin, God steps in, meting out judgment and fostering His righteous cause.

God did that in Joshua 7. Achan saw, coveted, and took things after God had commanded, "in any wise keep yourselves from the accursed thing" (Joshua 6:18). Achan's punishment was death by stoning for both him and his entire family. If such punishment was justice for Achan's personal disobedience, what would a king deserve when he forsook God's commandments and led his entire kingdom into vile, despicable idolatry?

King Ahab tried to place the burden of responsibility on Elijah's shoulders. "It's all your fault, Elijah. You have greatly troubled Israel."

Elijah put the blame where it belonged—right back on King Ahab. Elijah knew that the problem began with Ahab's father, Omri, who "did worse than all that were before him" (1 Kings 16:25). But Ahab had topped even his father, in that he did evil in God's sight above all that were before him! Elijah pointed the finger: "Ye have forsaken the commandments of the LORD, and thou hast followed Baalim." It is your fault, King Ahab, yours and your father's before you. God gave Elijah the upper hand here, and Elijah directed Ahab to gather all Israel, all the prophets of Baal, and the prophets of the groves to Mount Carmel.

Mount Carmel is picturesque, overlooking the Mediterranean Sea, a place of mild weather, and a spot favored by its inhabitants. The mist had probably kept the area from suffering too severely during the drought. Also, there had previously been an altar erected to God on this mount (1 Kings 18:30).

Elijah called for all Israel to be gathered, including 450 prophets of Baal and 400 prophets of the groves. The latter set up and carried on idol worship in groves of trees at various locations over the northern kingdom of Israel. They were under the authorization of Jezebel herself. It was said that they "eat at Jezebel's table" (1 Kings 18:19).

Imagine the preparation and turmoil of travel all across the land as the edict was obeyed. People walking or riding mules jostled along the crowded paths. King Ahab probably arrived in his royal chariot. At any rate, the king's word was law, and he had ordered attendance on Mount Carmel. No one was allowed to send regrets.

When all Israel had gathered, Elijah, wasting no time on formalities or niceties, immediately stated, in the form of a question, the reason for the gathering: "How long halt ye between two opinions?" (1 Kings 18:21).

And Elijah came unto all the people, and said, How long halt ye between two opinions? if the LORD be God, follow him: but if Baal, then follow him. And the people answered him not a word. Then said Elijah unto the people, I, even I only, remain a prophet of the LORD; but Baal's prophets are four hundred and fifty men. Let them therefore give us two bullocks; and let them choose one bullock for themselves, and cut it in pieces, and lay it on wood, and put no fire under: and I will dress the other bullock, and lay it on wood, and put no fire under.

1 KINGS 18:21–23

18

WILL YOU GO ON LIMPING?

1 KINGS 18:21

What a trial it can be to have a bum ankle. If I put my weight on it, ouch! If I constantly favor it, limping with my weight on the other leg, the good leg will eventually complain of the overwork. How long can I go on like this? Should I go to the orthopedist and allow him to put a cast on the injured limb so it has the opportunity to heal? How long will I procrastinate? How long will I struggle with my decision? Well, I don't know that I am willing to submit to a cast, so. . . . Elijah confronted the people of Israel and asked: "How long halt ye between two opinions?" (1 Kings 18:21).

The easy way out is simply to not make a decision. If I remain neutral, then I may do whatever I wish at the moment. I am not committed to this side or that. I am not expected to be any certain place at any particular time, nor to support any particular program. But that leaves me limping, still struggling with just where I do belong. There must be a choice: I cannot have one with the other. The choice is mine—the burden of proof. I am a free agent, except that I cannot step out without that telltale limp! I cannot serve both God and the world.

When I finally weary to exhaustion with the limp, the doctor will still be there, willing to provide the strengthening needed for restoration to health.

How long will I procrastinate? I cannot stand with one foot on either side of the line. Both sides cannot be right. I must choose my allegiance and follow my leader! It is absurd to try to worship Jehovah God plus anything else.

No man can serve two masters:
for either he will hate the one, and love the other;
or else he will hold to the one, and despise the other.
Ye cannot serve God and mammon.
MATTHEW 6:24

—⚋⚋—

19

NOT A WORD

1 KINGS 18:21

T he ball is in your court. Now is the time for you to respond, to let your testimony be known. What will you do? What will you say?

Elijah challenged the crowd (those 450 prophets of Baal, the 400 prophets of the groves, and all the kingdom of Israel) to make their choice.

> *If the LORD be God, follow him:*
> *but if Baal, then follow him.*
> 1 KINGS 18:21

What did they say? They answered him not a word. Not one individual in the crowd was willing to stand up and be counted for the LORD God.

This has happened to me, too. I blew it. There was a fine opening in the conversation, and I could have spoken about our Lord, but I did not say anything. Not a word.

I wonder if their faith was failing. After all, for three and one-half years they had watched their gardens, crops, and land dry up. They had probably traveled to distant streams, hoping water was running there but finding each as waterless as their own wells and lips. Their faith had been stretched to the limits. Just how far can one trust God, anyway? There was no evidence that God knew or cared to provide water for this land, for these parched-skinned people.

So they stood there, perhaps wondering, *Has Elijah lost his mind in the dearth?* And they answered him not a word.

What they did not consider was that God desired each individual to turn away from Baal and give allegiance to Him.

God challenges every heart to turn away from sin, to face Him, to follow Him. He desires to see my face, to hear my voice. I need to look Him right in the eye and affirm: Lord, You are God alone. You are God of all creation and God of my life. By Your grace I choose to follow You.

I need never be ashamed to make my allegiance to God public. I ought never be too frightened of humans to take a stand for eternal God, never too preoccupied to find time to honor and worship Him. Never do I want to have to confess that I had an opportunity to give reason for my faith but answered not a word.

And call ye on the name of your gods, and I will call on the name of the LORD: and the God that answereth by fire, let him be God. And all the people answered and said, It is well spoken.

And Elijah said unto the prophets of Baal, Choose you one bullock for yourselves, and dress it first; for ye are many.

And call on the name of your gods, but put no fire under. And they took the bullock which was given them, and they dressed it, and called on the name of Baal from morning even until noon, saying, O Baal, hear us. But there was no voice, nor any that answered. And they leaped upon the altar which was made.

And it came to pass at noon, that Elijah mocked them, and said, Cry aloud: for he is a god; either he is talking, or he is pursuing, or he is in a journey, or peradventure he sleepeth, and must be awaked. And they cried aloud, and cut themselves after their manner with knives and lancets, till the blood gushed out upon them. And it came to pass, when midday was past, and they prophesied until the time of the offering of the evening sacrifice, that there was neither voice, nor any to answer, nor any that regarded. 1 KINGS 18:24–29

20

THE GOD THAT ANSWERETH BY FIRE, LET HIM BE GOD

1 KINGS 18:24

The prophets of Baal were ready to prove their point. Their eyes were so blinded that they must have actually thought a man-carved image could and would hear their cries and do the impossible on their behalf.

Elijah had the floor. He stated that he was the only prophet of the LORD left. God had a secret of which Elijah was not aware: Elijah did not know about the other seven thousand godly men God had reserved and preserved during this time.

"Baal's prophets are four hundred fifty men," Elijah continued. "So let them give us two bullocks. Let Baal's prophets first choose one, cut it in pieces, and lay it on wood. But put no fire under! I will do the same with the second bullock. And the God that answereth by fire, let him be God" (see 1 Kings 18:22–24).

All the people answered, "It is well spoken."

Baal was known as the god of light or fire. Therefore, this was a fair demand from Elijah. Let Baal prove himself in his most renowned area of expertise.

That God could produce light and fire was not a foreign idea to the worshipers of Jehovah. Think of Moses' writings recounting Abel's sacrifice, God's call to Moses from a burning bush, the pillar of fire between Moses and the Israelites fleeing from Pharaoh's godless authority and pursuit. "He led them. . .all the night with a light of fire" (Psalm 78:14). God's presence was revealed at the giving of the Law on Mount Sinai, like a devouring fire. All through God's word are examples of God revealing His presence by appearing in or as fire. Yes, the God that answereth by fire, let Him be God!

Elijah stood alone before the 450 prophets of Baal.

I know where my inner peace is found—
That sure direction, inner calm:
It's not in fussing or fervored flight,

But in resting each moment in the
    Master's might.

Elijah spoke. He had stood before the king and before the destitute widow. In each instance, he spoke God's message boldly. Neither time had God failed to accomplish all that He promised through Elijah.

On Mount Carmel, one can sense calm assurance in Elijah's demeanor and directives. How unlike Baal's prophets and their frenzied activity following Elijah's pronouncement! All day they called aloud to their god, leaped upon the altar, and cut themselves with knives and lancets. What a bloody, revolting, pitiful sight!

At noon, Elijah suggested that their god was traveling, at war, or asleep and needed to be waked. They took the challenge, crying louder until the time for the evening sacrifice.

But the God of Elijah was and is living and hearing. Elijah asked, "Hear me, O LORD, hear me, that this people may know that thou art the LORD God, and that thou hast turned their heart back again" (1 Kings 18:37). That was Elijah's only goal. He wanted them to realize that what he had done was based upon the word of the living God.

ALL I HAVE NEEDED

Our soul waiteth for the LORD:
he is our help and our shield. . . .
Let none that wait on thee be ashamed.
PSALM 33:20; 25:3

Victory is not in giving way
to fear:
trying,
crying.

But victory is in grasping
faith:
trusting,
taking.

I came and claimed; I carried away all that I
needed for all of the day.

—∿—

And Elijah said unto all the people, Come near unto me. And all the people came near unto him. And he repaired the altar of the LORD that was broken down. And Elijah took twelve stones, according to the number of the tribes of the sons of Jacob, unto whom the word of the LORD came, saying, Israel shall be thy name: And with the stones he built an altar in the name of the LORD: and he made a trench about the altar, as great as would contain two measures of seed. And he put the wood in order, and cut the bullock in pieces, and laid him on the wood, and said, Fill four barrels with water, and pour it on the burnt sacrifice, and on the wood. And he said, Do it the second time. And they did it the second time. And he said, Do it the third time. And they did it the third time. And the water ran round about the altar; and he filled the trench also with water.

And it came to pass at the time of the offering of the evening sacrifice, that Elijah the prophet came near, and said, LORD God of Abraham, Isaac, and of Israel, let it be known this day that thou art God in Israel, and that I am thy servant, and that I have done all these things at thy word. Hear me, O LORD, hear me, that this people may know that thou art the LORD God, and that thou hast turned their heart back again.

1 KINGS 18:30–37

21

Pictures Speak Louder

Stand thou still a while,
that I may shew thee the word of God.
1 Samuel 9:27

The restless silence surrounding the crowd gathered around Elijah could be felt. The Baal worshipers had exhausted all the strength of their bodies and voices. They had given the determination of their combined wills to bring about a demonstration of the power of their god, but the god they called Baal was less than a mortal man who could leap and cry out and bleed. No one had regarded their passionate demands. They had crowned Baal their supreme deity, but it remained an inanimate creation of the hands of its worshipers.

Elijah called for the baffled, defeated, exhausted,

and purposeless people to come near. Hearing a word of instruction, they blindly followed it.

Elijah, employing no self-aggrandizement, repaired the broken-down altar of God that had long been on that mount. Taking twelve stones to symbolize the twelve tribes of Israel, he built an altar in the name of the LORD. Digging a trench around the altar, he purposely, steadily worked, laying wood in order on the altar, cutting the bullock into pieces, and placing it on top.

Then Elijah gave a strange command: Fill four barrels with water and pour it on the sacrifice. Beneath the mount was a spring. Possibly its water was consecrated to the LORD and not generally accessible to people, even in drought. The men had to descend the mount and haul the four barrels of water back up to the top. Elijah said, "Do it again!" Down the mountain; fill them up; haul them to the top again; pour them over the sacrifice. A third time Elijah repeated the command; a third time they repeated the task. The sacrifice was soggy, and the trench around the altar was filled with water, too.

Fill barrels with water and pour over all!
Do it again in everyone's sight!
Pour a third time, so no one will doubt
That sacrifice so soggy can never ignite!
Then pray with no selfish perspective in mind;

Pray that the glory of God be in view!
Ask "whatsoever" as God commands,
And, lo! God will be glorified through you.

It was the normal hour for the evening sacrifice. Elijah came before God at the altar and prayed that God would hear him, and all Israel would know that He is God.

> *The effectual fervent prayer*
> *of a righteous man availeth much.*
> JAMES 5:16

Elijah was probably oblivious to all else as he willingly carried out everything God directed. He was foolish, humanly speaking, to expect the totally impossible.

If we are going to let God be seen through us, we must be oblivious of hindrances, impossibilities, fears, and weaknesses. We must obey God's word in faith, even unto what would appear to men as foolishness.

Pictures do speak louder than words.

—∿—

Then the fire of the LORD fell, and consumed the burnt sacrifice, and the wood, and the stones, and the dust, and licked up the water that was in the trench. And when all the people saw it, they fell on their faces: and they said, The LORD, he is the God; the LORD, he is the God. And Elijah said unto them, Take the prophets of Baal; let not one of them escape. And they took them: and Elijah brought them down to the brook Kishon, and slew them there. 1 KINGS 18:38–40

22

DON'T LET ONE GET AWAY!

E lijah said the last word of his prayer, and fire dropped on the sacrifice. God's fire literally consumed the soggy sacrifice, the wood, stones, dust, and even all the water in the trench.

God had, with no possible doubt, shown Himself to be the LORD God. Elijah did not have to explain God and His power; the people saw with their own eyes. He did not have to remind the people to worship the LORD God; they fell on their faces and cried out, "The LORD, he is the God; the LORD, he is the God" (1 Kings 18:39).

If the people's hearts had sincerely turned to God, the priests of Baal were no longer needed. Only one could be God, so Elijah gave the command to kill them. Down to the brook Kishon went the determined Israelites in the wake of their declaration of God's deity. Down they went, dragging Baal's prophets to the end of their satanic ministry and the end of their earthly lives. They were carrying out God's Law:

> *If there arise among you a prophet. . .*
> *saying, Let us go after other gods,*
> *which thou hast not known,*
> *and let us serve them. . .that prophet. . .*
> *shall be put to death;*
> *because he hath spoken to turn you away*
> *from the LORD your God. . . .*
> *So shalt thou put the evil away*
> *from the midst of thee.*
> DEUTERONOMY 13:1–2, 5

They did not let one get away.

Whatever hinders wholehearted obedience to God must be seized and rendered helpless in Jesus' name. Don't let one get away!

And Elijah said unto Ahab, Get thee up, eat and drink; for there is a sound of abundance of rain. So Ahab went up to eat and to drink. And Elijah went up to the top of Carmel; and he cast himself down upon the earth, and put his face between his knees, and said to his servant, Go up now, look toward the sea. And he went up, and looked, and said, There is nothing. And he said, Go again seven times. And it came to pass at the seventh time, that he said, Behold, there ariseth a little cloud out of the sea, like a man's hand. And he said, Go up, say unto Ahab, Prepare thy chariot, and get thee down, that the rain stop thee not. And it came to pass in the mean while, that the heaven was black with clouds and wind, and there was a great rain. And Ahab rode, and went to Jezreel. And the hand of the LORD was on Elijah; and he girded up his loins, and ran before Ahab to the entrance of Jezreel.

1 KINGS 18:41–46

23

WHISPERS IN MY EAR

1 KINGS 18:41

The great victory on Mount Carmel was complete. God had triumphed over the prophets of Baal! Elijah fearlessly announced to King Ahab, "Get thee up, eat and drink; for there is a sound of abundance of rain" (1 Kings 18:41). Elijah's heart heard the rain coming from God's faithful hand, though others did not perceive it. God reveals His secrets to His servants who wait on Him.

My friend said, "The more you know God, the more you trust Him." The more you trust, the more you know Him, because God entrusts further confidences to you.

The secret of the LORD is
with them that fear him.
PSALM 25:14

First Samuel 9:15 records that the LORD, on the previous day, had told Samuel something in his ear. Think of that! A secret of God's heart was conveyed directly to a human heart in the normal way that friends share a secret: God whispered in Samuel's ear.

My God is alive! My God is my friend who walks, talks, and shares with me, and I with Him! He puts in my mind what I need to know, the direction I ought to go, and sometimes simply reminds me, "I love you so!"

Yes, the more I trust God, the more He trusts His secrets to me. The more God whispers in my ear through His Word, the more confidence I place in Him, and the more I find desire to obey Him and do fearlessly whatever He asks. In the doing, I realize God's provision, and my faith is strengthened and established.

How pleasant it is to hear the "whispers" of God in my ear! What wonders of sweet, satisfying companionship we share, eternal God and just me!

24

WAIT FOR
GOD'S SEVENTH TIME

1 KINGS 18:42–44

Elijah could almost feel the cool, wet freshness! He claimed God's word and boldly announced to the king that God was ready to drop His blessing on the parched earth. Then the king went to refresh himself with food and drink.

But Elijah went to the top of Mount Carmel, cast himself down upon the earth, and waited to receive God's promise. He had full freedom to ask for rain. That promise gave him incentive for praying, direction in prayer, and permission to expect rain from God. He bowed in submission to his understanding of God's will. With prayerful heart, he waited expectantly.

When we can only groan with perplexity and longings too deep for words, God's Holy Spirit takes our confusion and intercedes for us according to God's will. Oh, what salvation is ours—Christ living in us! Personal fellowship with God is ours because His Holy Spirit makes intercession for us!

The reiterated Law of God told the Israelites that if they would not hearken to the voice of the LORD their God to do all His commandments, God would make the heaven over their heads brass, the earth to be iron, and the rain powder and dust (Deuteronomy 28:23–24).

Elijah had been victorious in faith that day and had received miraculous answers to his prayer. Now he bowed before God and waited for Him to melt the heavens of brass and drop the refreshing rain. Not even raising his head or eyes, Elijah spoke to his servant from that humble posture, head bowed to the ground. "Go up now. Look toward the sea!"

Elijah's servant went up to look out over the Mediterranean Sea. Gazing into the clear blue sky, he saw nothing to suggest a hint of rain—no cloud, not even a slight haze to intimate the approach of a cloud. He felt nothing—no slight, cooling breeze. He heard nothing—no thunder, no raindrops. Nothing. That was all he had to report to Elijah: "There is nothing."

It appears Elijah never rose up, but from his posture of concurrence with God's will—there on the ground with his face between his knees—he instructed his servant to go seven times. When God does not give an answer to our prayers quickly, though we truly asked in faith believing, we must continue waiting expectantly. God does not lie, and He has promised that fervent prayer avails.

> *Men ought always to pray,*
> *and not to faint.*
> LUKE 18:1

Seven is God's number of completion—His perfect number. There were seven days in the week of creation. In God's overall plan for mankind, there are seven ages. At the start of each age, God revealed to men what He expected of them during that time. Each of the first five ages ended with man's failure to comply with God's instruction. The course of human events in the present age does nothing to foster hope that man's heart has changed from its normal deceit and desperate wickedness.

But we, too, wait for number seven! When our Lord's time is perfect, He will consummate this age by calling His own to His presence. Then we will be changed to be like Him and will be forever with Christ! Oh, the glory Christ's own will experience when His perfect time has come!

Even so, come, Lord Jesus.
REVELATION 22:20

Elijah's servant dutifully went again, and the third time, fourth, fifth, and sixth. The seventh time he must have returned as eager as a child for his promised ice cream. "Behold, there ariseth a little cloud out of the sea, like a man's hand" (1 Kings 18:44), he announced. It was only a little thing, just one little bit of white atop the endless blue expanse.

And he prayed again,
and the heaven gave rain,
and the earth brought forth her fruit.
JAMES 5:18

That was all Elijah needed, just a little sign that it was God's time to fulfill His promise and end the drought. He sent word to King Ahab to get down from the mountain. If one believes God is sending rain, it is wise to get to shelter! So Elijah ran like a gazelle, while clouds blackened, the wind arose, and a great rain began to pelt the dry earth.

Thou, O God, didst send a plentiful rain,
whereby thou didst confirm thine inheritance,
when it was weary.
PSALM 68:9

It can seem ever so long—that time between when I know God has heard and answered my prayer and that time when I actually hold the answer in my hands. The wait could seem seven times longer than I had hoped. Yet seven is God's perfect number, and God's timing is always perfect!

I will wait for God's perfect time, the moment He will give that which I have believed to be His will for me, that which I have by faith claimed for my own. Then, along with the widow clutching her resurrected son, I will know great strengthening of my faith, being assured beyond doubt that the Word of God is truth.

Wait! Wait! It is well worth the wait for God's seventh time.

PART 3

"CHOOSE YOU THIS DAY"

1 KINGS 19–2 KINGS 2:15

INTRODUCTION

What more could God ask of His servant? Elijah had trusted God to restore life to a dead boy. Then he had faced the nation, standing alone for God before the wicked king, heathen prophets, and citizens of all Israel. God had honored Elijah's prayers of faith with miracles of fire, the slaying of hundreds of prophets of Baal, and rain from a clear blue sky.

Now, in the wake of tremendous victories, Elijah finds himself intimidated by a threat on his life! He may be considering abandoning God's work. God will meet Elijah right where he is hiding and explain some further exploits in His plan for the prophet. Elijah will remain faithful to His God until the end of his life on earth. And *that* will be a most unusual event.

And Ahab told Jezebel all that Elijah had done,
and withal how he had slain all the prophets with
the sword. Then Jezebel sent a messenger unto
Elijah, saying, So let the gods do to me, and more
also, if I make not thy life as the life of one of them
by to morrow about this time. And when he saw
that, he arose, and went for his life, and came to
Beer-sheba, which belongeth to Judah, and left his
servant there. But he himself went a day's journey
into the wilderness, and came and sat down under
a juniper tree: and he requested for himself that he
might die; and said, It is enough; now, O LORD,
take away my life; for I am not better than my
fathers. And as he lay and slept under a juniper
tree, behold, then an angel touched him, and said
unto him, Arise and eat. And he looked, and,
behold, there was a cake baken on the coals, and a
cruse of water at his head. And he did eat and
drink, and laid him down again.

And the angel of the LORD *came again the*
second time, and touched him, and said, Arise and
eat; because the journey is too great for thee. And he
arose, and did eat and drink, and went in the
strength of that meat forty days and forty nights
unto Horeb the mount of God. And he came thither
unto a cave, and lodged there; and, behold, the
word of the LORD *came to him, and he said unto*
him, What doest thou here, Elijah?

And he said, I have been very jealous for the LORD God of hosts: for the children of Israel have forsaken thy covenant, thrown down thine altars, and slain thy prophets with the sword; and I, even I only, am left; and they seek my life, to take it away.

And he said, Go forth, and stand upon the mount before the LORD. And, behold, the LORD passed by, and a great and strong wind rent the mountains, and brake in pieces the rocks before the LORD; but the LORD was not in the wind: and after the wind an earthquake; but the LORD was not in the earthquake: and after the earthquake a fire; but the LORD was not in the fire: and after the fire a still small voice.   1 KINGS 19:1–12

25

When It's Time to Change

1 Kings 19:1

King Ahab stood with the prophets of Baal from the time he took Jezebel to wife. God's word says he did evil in the sight of the LORD, more than all who were before him. Now, God's prophet Elijah had fearlessly stood before Ahab and all Israel, declaring, "If the LORD be God, follow him: but if Baal, then follow him" (1 Kings 18:21).

It was time—yes, and far past time—for King Ahab to make a change. It was time for him to own the truth and lead the people of his kingdom into the truth of God.

When God used Elijah to speak His words and honored His prophet's faith by sending fire from heaven, miracles abounded right before the eyes of King Ahab and his 450 prophets of Baal, the prophets of the grove, and all Israel. No one could deny what they had actually seen.

Those people all fell on their faces in terror, saying, "The LORD, he is the God" (1 Kings 18:39).

But King Ahab was not into change. He went back to the palace to eat and drink and to tell the story of the day to Jezebel. He told all that Elijah had done. He only saw what he wanted to see— the man Elijah. Though the events that transpired on the mountain could never be effected by any man—or all the men of earth combined—the king reported all that Elijah had done. All the king's subjects saw God in power on the mount, bowed low in humbleness, and confessed with their mouths, "The LORD, he is the God."

But the king's heart must have been so hardened through his devotion to Baal for the past twenty years or so that he found within himself no desire to change. Nothing in Scripture indicates that he contemplated the possibility, even after all he had viewed that day. He was the king. He was intelligent. But he had a queen named Jezebel who tended to exercise authority over everything, including the king. Perhaps he feared her and her ruthless power.

Whatever King Ahab's understanding, after such demonstration as God had given that day, he should have been on his knees begging God for mercy.

Yet how much difference do I find in my own heart today? God reveals some discrepancy between His perfect will and my walk. I may try to ignore Him, or I may attempt to gloss over what He is revealing. I may minimize or even deny the truth, or try to talk my way out of this, rationalizing that for me it is all right.

If God says it's time to change something, I had better consider Who is speaking. I need to be willing to do all His will with all my heart. When I do, He gives peace, joy, and thankfulness for the victory He provided for me.

I wonder how the king felt as he returned home and explained to Jezebel what had taken place.

26

Don't Look at
What You See!

1 Kings 19:1–2

Jezebel sent a threatening message to Elijah when
her husband told her all that Elijah had done on
Mount Carmel.

Jezebel was furious because Elijah had commanded all "her" prophets of Baal to be slain. Her
threat to Elijah was, "So let the gods do to me, and
more also, if I make not thy life as the life of one
of them by to morrow about this time" (1 Kings
19:2). She allowed twenty-four hours for her abhor-
rent plan to be brought to fulfillment, and it looks as
if she fully expected to carry out her threat. Certainly she would not bloody her own two hands. She
had countless loyal subjects to fulfill her every
whim; her command was law. Her threat would be
carried out.

That is if someone could find Elijah.

When God determines to protect His own servant, none on earth or in heaven is able to take that servant's life.

> My times are in God's hand, even my
>   death is in His plan. . .
> Unless His scheduled coming to take us
>   into glory
> Foils Satan's ploy and snatches us into joy!
> Oh, quickly come, Lord Jesus! My times
>   are as Thou pleaseth.

When Jesus walked on the raging water out to the disciples' ship (as recorded in Matthew 14), the waves meant nothing to Him. He had a goal in mind, a purpose to fulfill. His focus was on the end result. Nothing around Him entered into consideration.

Peter desired to walk on the water, too, and at Jesus' command, he did! But then he looked at the storm blowing around them and became fearful. He should have kept his eyes on the Lord of the sea; he should not have looked at what was going on around him in the world. Sight hindered his faith.

Jesus upbraided Peter: "O thou of little faith, wherefore didst thou doubt?" (Matthew 14:31).

Elijah had a similar problem: He saw in his mind what Jezebel was threatening to do to him, and that sight hindered his faith.

While we look not at the things which are seen,
but at the things which are not seen:
for the things which are seen are temporal;
but the things which are not seen are eternal.
2 CORINTHIANS 4:18

Oh, Elijah, what are you doing running away in fear of a wicked queen? Have you forgotten that God is God? Don't you remember His mighty, visible answers to your prayer of faith in recent days? Your God has not changed in the least; He will not fail you or forsake you. You well know Whom you have believed, and surely after all your experiences these past three years, you cannot doubt the love, faithfulness, and power of your God.

But Elijah was bone weary and emotionally depleted. He was just plain tired of the battle. Heedless of thought or of seeking God's directive for him at that point, he took off on the run.

He ran about eighty miles to Beer-sheeba in Judah, out of Jezebel's realm of authority. There he left his servant. Then he went a day's journey into the wilderness, sat down under a juniper tree, and requested that God would take his life. He had decided this was the right time for him to die. The battle at Mount Carmel was fought and won. Maybe Elijah felt that he had accomplished enough for God and deserved a break. Was he still looking around him instead of looking up?

I wonder why Elijah ran all those miles to escape death and then asked to die. Was it a cry of desperation in his exhaustion? Instead of death, God simply provided a lone tree to give him some shade, and gave him sleep to bring restoration of strength and stamina. Elijah fell asleep under the juniper bush.

27

CAN GOD?

1 KINGS 19:1–4

In a reiteration of the Israelites' wilderness wanderings, Asaph in Psalm 78 relates that the Israelites asked, "Can God furnish a table in the wilderness?" (v. 19). The Israelites had already satisfied their thirst with water that God sent out of a rock and their hunger with manna—bread straight from heaven. They ate angel's food, yet they did not believe God or trust in His salvation, wisdom, and love. Because their hearts were not right with God, He consumed their days in vanity and their years in trouble. He consumed them "in emptiness, falsity and futility," says The Amplified Bible in Psalm 78:33.

Elijah had stood through thick and thin with God for about three and one-half years, speaking before the king, waiting by the brook in solitude, and following on to Zarephath and the home of a destitute widow, where God miraculously gave daily bread. God had also trusted him with the burden of the widow's son's dead body, faithfully restoring the lad's life in response to Elijah's faith.

On the mount, Elijah had, with no hint of fear or disbelief, faced the king, the false prophets, and the entire nation. He openly, boldly trusted God to do the impossible. Therefore all who had gathered saw the miraculous works of God: fire that consumed not only the sacrifice, but also the stones, dust, and water. Some fire! Most unnatural.

Nevertheless, in the wake of such mighty, miraculous masteries, Elijah sat under a lone juniper tree. He had run over eighty miles to get out of Jezebel's realm of rule, gone on a day's journey into the wilderness, and sat down to ask God to let him die. He was likely depressed, emotionally and physically expended from the contest on the mount and the lonely trek to his desert hideaway.

It does not seem possible that Elijah could doubt God's ability to preserve his life. His body had been kept safe, and he had eaten every day. It also seems obvious that he had held conversations with God and thus was never without Someone to talk to. But his emotional strength was worn to the place where he was simply ready to stop fighting. He was so weary that he prayed to die: "It is enough; now, O LORD, take away my life; for I am not better than my fathers" (1 Kings 19:4).

Can God also bless me with the desire to live, the desire to go on serving Him, when I have given and given and given of self until I feel as though there is nothing more left to give? Yes! Definitely, yes. My times are in God's hand, and He will constantly provide all I need for as long as He has planned for me to live on earth.

I wonder what Elijah would have thought if he had known God's plan for him included about ten more years life on earth. Would he have thoughtfully considered:

- Can God give me the will to go on with life?
- Can God keep this old body going that long?
- Why, LORD? Why not take me to Yourself? Why not now?

Regarding difficult times, my friend said, "You don't rejoice in what's happening; you rejoice in God Himself, and He gives you strength." He also gives hope and the goal of doing His pleasure.

So Elijah got up and did what God told him to do next: Go anoint Hazael to be king of Syria. That is all anyone needs to do—obey God's present direction; get up and go, leaving the "Why?" with God. If God has not revealed why, then we do not need to know. Where God leads, He always provides. We can do all things through Him.

In the strength God provides,
In the wisdom with which He guides,
Lay your plans as He will show,
Then confidently step out and go!

I wonder what Elijah's reaction would have been if God had told him at this time that he would be only the second person since the creation of the world who would never die. The first was Enoch, who so closely walked with God for 365 years that one day God simply translated him from earth to heaven.

When shall I fear,
When shall I dread
What may take place
In my life ahead?
Only when my LORD
Has ceased caring for me,
And that I know
Can never be.

"And Enoch walked with God: and he was not; for God took him" (Genesis 5:24). What a way to go—just walking hand in hand with your dearest friend and going right on home with that friend to stay forever.

The Hope Set Before Us

I walked today with Jesus, and our fellowship was blest;
I longed to continue with Him in that joy,
 for I love Him best.

Then He said, "Why not come home with
 me, for I love you so, my friend,
And all of My Father's love and home will
 be ours together, without end."

Then we walked right on, His hand clasp-
 ing mine and leading me all the way;
We walked, delighting in oneness, right on
 into eternal day.

28

CHERITH CALM

1 KINGS 19:3

Family members and friends—every one is loved, a precious gift from God, a treasure to my heart. Each is of comfort, companionship, and cheer to me in his or her own special way. It is the greatest of pleasures when we share God's word and God's working in our lives. We can also come to God in prayer together and know that fellowship of kindred minds that must be about as close as we can get to heaven while we still live here.

Each individual stands or falls before his Lord and Master. Each one shall give account of himself to God. In order for each of us to grow in God's likeness and love, time alone with God is essential. Yes, there definitely must be time to seek God alone. We must leave the company of family and friends, entertainment and errands, work and worry to seek God Himself.

In this frightening solitary time, while running for his life, Elijah left his servant, his one human companion, behind in Beer-sheba. He had to be all alone with God to seek God's direction and help without distraction.

It seems that Elijah had plenty of solitary places and spaces where he could get far enough from the daily grind to hear the voice of God. There was Cherith and Zarephath, and now here is another place where God will hide him.

Sometimes I have trouble finding any time or place where I can get away from it all. But I must make that effort to seek God's time and God's "there"—the place where He has determined to open His heart to me.

If I am going to hear what God the Lord would speak, I must plan, prepare, and put myself there. I want to hear His voice with no distraction. At times, that quiet place is only in my heart, but if I am listening, God's voice may be heard during the wildest tempest that floods over my life. If I will but open the ears of my heart to His voice, that still, small voice can drown out the entire world and fill my heart with purpose and peace.

Such quiet "Cherith calm" may be within my heart even during a Mount Carmel-like confrontation.

—m—

29

IT IS ENOUGH!

1 KINGS 19:4

It is enough. I cannot hang in there any longer. I am weary, worn out, fresh out of desire to continue striving from day to day. God, don't You want to get me out of this despondency? I cannot handle life! Please take me *home*.

This letdown feeling, a deep depression after a great victory, is not unusual. After the adrenaline has rushed like a flood and I have been carried along on the swells of the waves, suddenly I am sitting all alone on the sand.

It is all over now. That goal for which I struggled has been reached; that challenge that seemed impossible has been met and conquered. Suddenly I feel as though I have no purpose for being and no strength or incentive to look ahead, set a new goal, and plan how to reach it.

That is when the enemy comes in like a flood,

153

when I am most vulnerable. Unless I lean hard upon my God, I will give way to the false ideas the enemy of our souls presents. I will say, "I can't. It's too hard." I will admit I don't even want to try.

It looks like that is what happened to Elijah. After reaching the pinnacle of trust in God and openly standing with all boldness before the idol worshipers, he took his eyes off God. He became terrified that Jezebel might kill him, and his fear carried him eighty miles on foot.

At last, all alone, safe from the threat of death at Jezebel's hand, he conversed with his God. It comes naturally for a believer to talk with God about everything. Right now Elijah's deepest need, as he understood it, was to die. He could find within himself no more strength to battle, no more desire to go on.

But God found Elijah. In fact, God knew all the time where he was and what he was doing.

It is not impossible to rest and be refreshed and strengthened with desire to go on, to set new goals, to lay out plans for reaching them, and to get up and head in their direction!

God desires that I be established and strengthened in the truth, in faith, in His grace, and in my service for Him.

IT IS ENOUGH!

He brought me up also out of an horrible pit,
out of the miry clay,
and set my feet upon a rock,
and established my goings.
PSALM 40:2

Establishment is accomplished, as is every grace in my life, by God's working as a result of my faith. If I do not believe, I will not be firmly settled in God's will and way.

If ye will not believe,
surely ye shall not be established.
ISAIAH 7:9

Elijah asked that he might die, but God still had a very important assignment for him. There was yet a protégé to whom he must be an example, and he was to anoint that protégé, Elisha, to be God's next prophet.

God told him to do that anointing. He also reassured Elijah that he was not all alone: There were still seven thousand people in Israel who were faithful to God and had not bowed to Baal.

God's word is suited to my need at the current time. He knows how much I can handle—He is my Father! He has designed a future that will help me grow in His likeness. He has also given hope, sure and steadfast, of eternal life in His presence after this earthly life is completed. Every thought of God toward me is peace, not evil. My heavenly Father is constantly teaching me to grow in grace and knowledge of Himself. My future is as secure as the God of all the universe could make it. God is my Rock.

That is enough, oh, Lord! I will confidently accept the options You have selected for me. I do not need to know what will be tomorrow. But if tomorrow comes, I know already that, with You in control, it will be good.

—⦚—

30

INSTEAD OF
BLURTED-OUT WORDS

1 KINGS 19:5–8

When our physical bodies are demanding nourishment and rest and we cannot keep on as we are, we may find ourselves asking to die. God does answer prayer, yet we know not what to pray for as we ought. We may be at our wits' end physically and emotionally, not thinking clearly, not able to decide wisely.

God the Holy Spirit always intercedes on our behalf. He takes not only our words, but the very desires of our hearts, and conveys them to the Father. God knows when we cannot handle life.

He knoweth our frame;
he remembereth that we are dust.
PSALM 103:14

He knows that, in the heat of the battle, we sometimes say things that we really do not mean, ask for things that we really would not desire if we could see the end result of having them. We may only be voicing a desperate cry for help.

God, Who always answers prayer, grants the answer to our hearts' pleading, instead of the words we blurted out under the pressure of our circumstances. He knows the true desire of our hearts.

The old hymn "Praise Ye the Lord, the Almighty" questions: "Hast thou not seen how thy desires e'er have been granted in what He ordaineth?"

God's angel messenger came to the overwrought Elijah as he slept in the wilderness of Beer-sheba under the juniper tree. The angel touched him and said, "Rise and eat."

Elijah was so sleepy that he was not alert to the provider of his repast. He simply ate, drank, and went back to sleep. That was all right. It is good to sleep when body and mind need refreshing and rest. It is God's provision for our rejuvenation.

A second time God sent His angel, this time with an additional message. "Arise and eat; because the journey is too great for thee." The messenger knew something Elijah did not know or had not acknowledged: God was not through with him yet! God always knows what the future holds: Elijah was going on another journey.

He had farther to go on his life's journey. Instead of letting Elijah lie there feeling sorry for himself and giving his mind to thoughts he would be better off not to contemplate, God had work for him to do and places for him to go. The first assignment was a journey to Mount Horeb, where God was going to meet His servant with instructions.

Elijah traveled forty days, about two hundred miles, living off the cake and water that the angel had brought to him under the juniper tree. He must have become very hungry, yet God enabled him to keep on going, even though He sent no additional food. Why did God want Elijah hungry?

According to Leon Wood, in *Elijah, Prophet of God,* "God saw it as most conducive to making Elijah a proper recipient for what was in store for him on Mount Horeb. He needed to be made humble and teachable, and it is lack of life's provisions which works to this end, and not plenty."

When I am unable to meet my own needs, I must cast myself on the mercy of God and trust His faithfulness. God has already promised that, if I cast my burden upon Him, He will sustain.

I recall a miserable day when I was downhearted, depressed, and discouraged. I asked the Lord if I could call my dear friend to ask for prayer help. Rather than allowing me to do that, God led me to ask Him to lay it on my friend's heart to pray for me. He cast me totally upon Himself, and He totally met my need.

> My God has cast me on Himself,
> But what other place to be
> Than leaning on the heart of Him
> Who died and lives for me?

31

SHHH!

God had a lodging place, a cave, ready for Elijah's shelter at Mount Horeb. This is probably Mount Sinai, or part of it, the mount where God gave the Ten Commandments to His servant, Moses. Now again the word of the LORD came to this mount, to His servant Elijah. God's Word can discover me no matter how deep or how dark the cave where I hide.

God asked, "What are you doing here, Elijah?" Elijah's answer disclosed much, though he did not put it in exact words. He was feeling all alone, feeling his faithfulness to God was not being requited, and he was still afraid of Jezebel.

But what was he doing there, when God had not sent him there?

It seems God was offering His open heart to welcome Elijah's confession of self-pity and self-imposed travel. But all Elijah did was boast of his personal accomplishments and complain of his personal hardships.

See what I have done? See how faithful I am? No one else is as true to You as I am, LORD. And I'm scared! There was the crux of the problem: Elijah feared what men could do to him.

God told him to go forth and stand upon the mount before the LORD.

Hear the quiet! Absolute stillness captures attention more rapidly than any word, sound, or signal. Our world is so busy and ever so noisy. Shhh! God's voice is not usually heard in the rumble of traffic or in the confusion of rush, but in the quietness of a seeking heart.

To hear God's voice, I must be expecting Him to speak to me at any moment. I must be tuned to the correct channel, that is, turned away from sin and self. If I let myself get caught up in the world around me, my inner ear may not be attentive to His voice. God ministered to His servant Elijah when he was weary. He allowed sleep, gave food, and more sleep. This went on for a period of time not specified in Scripture, but it was sufficient time for Elijah's refreshment. The Word says he went in the strength of that refreshment for forty days.

I find it encouraging to see how God has numbered the days of testing. I need to take time to notice how He has provided refreshment during stressful times. I recognize that God's provision has always been enough to meet my spiritual, physical, and emotional needs of the moment! I can look up: God is! Shhh! I will listen! God speaks to an attentive heart.

Following rest and refreshment, there were great, bold, noisy, and captivating wonders for Elijah to behold. A wind of tornado force caused the mountain to vibrate. Huge boulders were loosened and fell crashing and splitting. The sound must have been deafening. Elijah did not seem to notice that God was doing this; he only saw the results of the fierce winds—the fragments.

Then there was an earthquake, and what does anyone think about at such a time except fear and personal safety and wondering, *Am I going to die now?*

The earthquake likely caused the mountain to vibrate even more violently than had the wind. Elijah felt the rock beneath his feet shudder and shake, watched as rocks tumbled and crumbled into gravel at his feet and huge cracks and crevices burst open. I can see Elijah in the calm moment when the quake ceased, possibly gazing down into a yawning chasm next to his feet.

Finally there was a fire. This ought to have grabbed Elijah's undivided attention, bringing remembrance of the recent fire on the mount, a fire that even consumed stones and drank up water, yet was completely in God's control. This time God was not in the fire. It was only a part of the means God used to disconcert Elijah, unsettle his self-possession, and thereby get his full attention. It was real fire, bright and hot. Perhaps its heat drove Elijah back into his cave.

Elijah was in the desert wilderness where the Israelites once wandered. He was far away from Jezreel, and was within the jurisdiction of a very good king, Jehoshaphat. This was a place where one would expect ever-constant solitude and never a disturbance by anything other than the constant heat of the sun's rays or a slight movement of the stifling air, or perhaps a bird winging across the blue, blue sky.

Elijah was surrounded by peaks of red rock, tier above tier. There he heard the howling wind, he felt the very rocks beneath his feet shudder and shake. As the earth quaked, he saw the fragments of those rocks tumbling, tumbling until the rocks had become gravel scattered over the sand. Then came the fire, which must have gotten Elijah's attention, for he heard God speak in a still, small voice.

> *He will speak peace unto his people,*
> *and to his saints:*
> *but let them not turn again to folly.*
> PSALM 85:8

And it was so, when Elijah heard it, that he wrapped his face in his mantle, and went out, and stood in the entering in of the cave. And, behold, there came a voice unto him, and said, What doest thou here, Elijah? And he said, I have been very jealous for the LORD God of hosts: because the children of Israel have forsaken thy covenant, thrown down thine altars, and slain thy prophets with the sword; and I, even I only, am left; and they seek my life, to take it away.

And the LORD said unto him, Go, return on thy way to the wilderness of Damascus: and when thou comest, anoint Hazael to be king over Syria: and Jehu the son of Nimshi shalt thou anoint to be king over Israel: and Elisha the son of Shaphat of Abel-meholah shalt thou anoint to be prophet in thy room. And it shall come to pass, that him that escapeth the sword of Hazael shall Jehu slay: and him that escapeth from the sword of Jehu shall Elisha slay. Yet I have left me seven thousand in Israel, all the knees which have not bowed unto Baal, and every mouth which hath not kissed him.

So he departed thence, and found Elisha the son of Shaphat, who was plowing with twelve yoke of oxen before him, and he with the twelfth: and Elijah passed by him, and cast his mantle upon him. And he left the oxen, and ran after Elijah, and said, Let me, I pray thee, kiss my father and my mother, and then I will follow thee. And he said unto him, Go back *again: for what have I done to thee? And he returned back from him, and took a yoke of oxen, and slew them, and boiled their flesh with the instruments of the oxen, and gave unto the people, and they did eat. Then he arose, and went after Elijah, and ministered unto him.* 1 KINGS 19:13–21

32

HE WRAPPED HIS FACE

1 KINGS 19:13

At the soft but steady voice of God, Elijah did two things. First he wrapped his face in his mantle. The Word does not say that he wrapped his shoulders, but when he heard God's voice, he covered his face. God's voice was hushed, calm. John R. MacDuff explains it as "the tremulous cadence of sweet music falling on the entranced ear."

Feel the serenity after the roaring storms of crumbling, tumbling rocks! Feel the stillness after the great, strong wind! Experience the silent, calming presence of God Himself.

His face wrapped up in the mantle, Elijah stepped to the door of his cave. He was wise to go hear what God wanted to tell him. What did the voice say? We are not told that any word was spoken. But oh, with what silent, stunning shout did

God make His presence known to His servant!

Rather than a greeting, rather than "How are you?" rather than a scolding, God asked a simple question that put the requisite of response upon the self-pitying prophet. "What are you doing here, Elijah?"

Elijah had been nursing his fear of being slain and had requested of God that he might die. He had slept a long time, eaten angel-prepared food, traveled for forty days to Horeb, and was living there in a cave. What he was doing in that cave was having a pity party for himself.

Ultimately, Elijah was still running away from the threats of wicked Jezebel. He was still feeling sorry for himself and feeling all alone. He was probably feeling put upon. The onus was on him, he claimed, to run far and fast enough to be safe from Jezebel's death threat.

Elijah declared to God how faithful he had been to His work and how all the other prophets had been slain. He whined to God, "I, even I only, am left; and they seek my life, to take it away" (1 Kings 19:10).

I wonder if Elijah, back there years ago when he was alone by the brook, entertained "poor me" from time to time. Here, after God's miraculous display, he was whimpering to God. Then God showed him the only remedy for self-pitying thoughts: Hear God's word!

God had Elijah's attention now, and He spoke in a still, small voice, a whisper that brought calm to Elijah's heart. God laid out the work He wanted Elijah to do. He also assured Elijah that he was not alone in his faith. There were in Israel seven thousand others who had eschewed Baal worship and remained true to God.

Elijah had no time for "poor me" now, for he had heard God's word. Following God's instructions, he went to the work.

When I am drowning in self-pity, I will wrap my heart in the mantle of God's love so I can see nothing around me. I will listen with my heart to the voice of God, and I will be obedient to God's word.

In pleasant weather, the traveler would toss the mantle over his shoulders. What a comfortable item to have at hand as one walked over the countryside! The mantle was large enough that one could wrap himself in it at night. It was a square cloth blanket or, if a prophet's mantle, it was a sheepskin. Likely, it was all a poor person would have for covering. Moses' Law instructed that if it were given as collateral, it had to be returned to the owner by the time the sun went down. It was the poor man's protection from the night chill.

The mantle was versatile. When the children

of Israel rose up to follow Moses in fleeing from Pharaoh, the women took their kneading troughs (probably large, shallow pottery or wooden bowls) with bread dough in them and wrapped the entire trough in their mantles for carrying.

All our heavy burdens are shouldered by the loving care of our heavenly Father. They are in that mantle of His love—everlasting, changeless love for His own.

J. R. MacDuff, in *Streams in the Desert,* offers this calming word: "Oh, happy are we if the hurricanes that ripple life's unquiet sea have the effect of making Jesus more precious. Better the storm with Christ than smooth waters without Him."

33

LISTEN UP!

1 KINGS 19:13–14

God asked Elijah once more, after he had witnessed a magnificent demonstration of God's power, "What doest thou here, Elijah?" God knew Elijah's name and his game. Elijah reiterated his well-rehearsed sob story, word for word. He briefly and rightly condemned the actions of the children of Israel who had turned themselves to Baal worship, but mainly he reminded God that he, Elijah, had been ever so faithful to God. He alone!

"And they seek my life to take it away!" he lamented.

After the rocking earthquake, the relentless wind, the raging fire, after hearing God's calming voice, Elijah still felt sorry for Elijah.

It is hard to triumph over the doldrums, and God's children are not exempt from the frailties and failures of humanity. But God, having work for His servant to do, did not acknowledge Elijah's complaint. He knew that Elijah's greatest need was another interest, something to cause him to focus on God and His word of instruction and the task that God would assign to him. God wrapped the mantle of His love around Elijah.

Oh, how pleasant it is to never be apart from the comforting love of God! He covers us, carries us, and comforts us just because He so loves us. Lord, next time I feel "poor me" coming on, please help me to remember to rest and rejoice in You.

Victory!

At a time when your little world is shaken
And life seems to be going awry,
You live and you breathe of necessity,
But life seems to be passing you by.
Nothing makes any sense or matters;
Who cares anyway how you feel?
No one would understand your explanation
How depression o'er mind and body can steal.
At such a time there is only one answer,
Only one source of true help and aid:
The answer is "God-become-one-of-us."
Every burden on Him may be laid.
Over and again I've gone down to the bottom,
Where no hope and no strength I could find.
Over and again I was lifted, when I claimed it:
I praised God and victory was mine!

When they began to sing and to praise,
the LORD. . .
made them to rejoice over their enemies. . .
God gave. . .rest round about.
2 CHRONICLES 20:22, 27, 30

34

SOLD OUT TO ETERNAL GOD

1 KINGS 19:15–21

God included in His instructions to Elijah that he was to anoint Hazael to be the new king of Syria and Jehu the new king of Israel. What was to come of invincible, godless King Ahab?

Then God said, "Elisha. . .shalt thou anoint to be prophet in thy room." The Word was definite in announcing the fact that Elijah's ministry as God's prophet was drawing toward its conclusion. But Elijah had lived in bold public testimony of God's power, and God had public purposes still to be fulfilled through him.

God continued in answer to Elijah's unspoken words, those suppositions that were masked in complaints: "I, even I only. . . ." Why had God not brought His own causes to a rightful end? All Israel had not turned back to God, though Elijah had been sold out to God and faithfully carried out His word.

God revealed that not only would Elijah anoint Jehu to be the new king and Elisha the prophet, but that Kings Hazael and Jehu would slay the godless ones. Those that escaped their swords, Elisha would slay. Vengeance belongs to God alone.

> *Know. . .that the LORD thy God, he is God,*
> *the faithful God, which keepeth. . .*
> *mercy with them that love him and keep his*
> *commandments to a thousand generations;*
> *and repayeth them that hate him to their face,*
> *to destroy them. . . .*
> DEUTERONOMY 7:9–10

Elijah got up and acted upon the instructions God had given him, departing from the cave on Mount Horeb to find Elisha.

Elisha was busy at work, plowing a field with the last of twelve yoke of oxen. We are not told if Elisha was weary of the work in which he was engaged or if he longed to do something else. Maybe he was a contented farmer, doing faithfully what God had placed before him. As Elijah went past, he threw his mantle on Elisha. Elisha immediately received this as a token of God's calling in his life. He was ready to listen and follow God's word.

When Elijah threw his mantle on Elisha, he was offering him friendship, care, and instruction. From this moment until Elijah's going to heaven, Elisha served Elijah. They were now one in spirit, since they shared the same mantle. Elisha also shared in Elijah's honor.

Elisha ran after Elijah and requested a bit of time to dutifully say good-bye to his father and mother. We are not given any background information regarding Elisha's age or place of birth, but he was likely still young at this time. Since he was plowing along with eleven others, the family was most likely one of means.

Elijah allowed Elisha to do what he needed in regard to his father and mother—or to go back to his occupation and forget the incident altogether. God wants us to serve Him willingly, not out of constraint. But Elisha had heard God calling and was ready, even eager, to follow. He was doing God's will when he was farming. Now God had new service for him, and he appears to be pleased by his call, making a farewell feast of boiled oxen for his family.

In Exodus, Moses gave instructions to the congregation regarding donating necessities for the tabernacle where they would worship God. Moses said, "Whosoever is of a willing heart, let him bring it, an offering" (Exodus 35:5). Men and women came who were willing hearted, wise hearted, whose hearts stirred them up to serve God in this way. They gladly brought an offering to God.

Elisha, in the same spirit of willing, hearty obedience, responded to the call to serve the LORD. He, too, departed to do God's will. I wonder if Elijah was pleased to have a human companion for the last days of his life, one who loved God and wanted to learn to be His prophet.

Elisha went after Elijah, followed him, and served him. He poured water on Elijah's hands, we are told in 2 Kings 3:11. No service is too commonplace for one who is sold out to eternal God. No service is unnoticed or forgotten by God.

And Ahab said to Elijah, Hast thou found me, O mine enemy? And he answered, I have found thee: because thou hast sold thyself to work evil in the sight of the LORD. Behold, I will bring evil upon thee, and will take away thy posterity. . . . And will make thine house like the house of Jeroboam the son of Nebat, and like the house of Baasha the son of Ahijah, for the provocation wherewith thou hast provoked me to anger, and made Israel to sin.

And of Jezebel also spake the LORD, saying, The dogs shall eat Jezebel by the wall of Jezreel. Him that dieth of Ahab in the city the dogs shall eat; and him that dieth in the field shall the fowls of the air eat.

But there was none like unto Ahab, which did sell himself to work wickedness in the sight of the LORD, whom Jezebel his wife stirred up. And he did very abominably in following idols, according to all things as did the Amorites, whom the LORD cast out before the children of Israel.

1 KINGS 21:20–21; 22–26

35

SOLD OUT TO EVIL

1 KINGS 20–21

King Ahab warred against Syria, and the Bible states he "smote the horses and chariots, and slew the Syrians with a great slaughter" (1 Kings 20:21). This was done at God's command to Ahab through a prophet. God was demonstrating to Ahab, "I am the LORD."

There was a second campaign against Syria that resulted in King Ahab's sparing the life of the Syrian king, even though the LORD had appointed King Ben-hadad to utter destruction. God then sent a prophet to King Ahab with the promise that his life would go for Ben-hadad's life.

King Ahab continued in his wicked ways. He coveted the vineyard of Naboth and, being refused a trade for or purchase of it, he went to his bed pouting.

Now who could better get their own way than Jezebel? She consoled her husband with a promise to obtain the vineyard he desired, and then she devised a scheme to have Naboth stoned to death. When her vile plot was carried out, she gleefully went to her husband with the word that he should get up and go possess the vineyard, for Naboth was dead. Leaving off his pouting, he got up and went to possess "his" vineyard.

The word of the LORD came again to God's prophet Elijah, instructing him to go to Naboth's vineyard and clueing him in as to what had taken place regarding Naboth and King Ahab. He sent Elijah with a warning for the king. "Thus saith the LORD, In the place where dogs licked the blood of Naboth shall dogs lick thy blood, even thine" (1 Kings 21:19).

"Hast thou found me, O mine enemy?" was King Ahab's response. Elijah was only Ahab's enemy because the king had chosen to be the enemy of God.

Boldly Elijah explained: "I have found thee: because thou hast sold thyself to work evil in the sight of the LORD" (1 Kings 21:20). Elijah told him that since he had killed and taken possession of Naboth's property, he, too, would lose his life, all his posterity would be cut off, and Jezebel would come to a vile death, being eaten by dogs.

SOLD OUT TO EVIL

But there was none like unto Ahab,
which did sell himself to work wickedness
in the sight of the LORD,
whom Jezebel his wife stirred up.
And he did very abominably in following idols. . . .
1 KINGS 21:25–26

And it came to pass, when Ahab heard those words, that he rent his clothes, and put sackcloth upon his flesh, and fasted, and lay in sackcloth, and went softly.

And the word of the LORD came to Elijah the Tishbite, saying, Seest thou how Ahab humbleth himself before me? because he humbleth himself before me, I will not bring the evil in his days: but in his son's days will I bring the evil upon his house.

1 KINGS 21:27–29

36

THE BITTER END

1 KINGS 21:27–29

God's word really moved King Ahab. He tore his clothes, put on sackcloth, and fasted. He "went softly," the Bible says.

I may put on the costume of a princess with all its finery. Outwardly, I might look like a princess, but that would not make me a princess. I would just be plain me in a masquerade. So King Ahab put on a show of one penitent over his sin, but reading the account of his life, we know that his heart had not changed. He hated one of God's faithful prophets, Micaiah; he did not restore the vineyard to Naboth's heirs; and he did not forsake his idols. It looked to men that he was repentant, but he was not sold out to God by any means.

Yet since he gave some glory to God by humbling himself, God blessed him and promised that the king would not experience the ruin of his house. That would come to pass in the next generation. God's tender mercy was yet open to this poor sinner.

> Oh, what depth of mercy
> In the heart of eternal God!
> Oh, what breadth of pardon
> For the soul obeying His Word!
> Oh, what length of lovingkindness,
> Reaching to the vilest offender,
> Lifting unto full salvation
> That soul by His gracious favor!

King Ahab's example gives a possible reason why the wicked prosper. "God rewards their external service with external mercies," says Matthew Henry.

I am encouraged to heartily sell out to God, desiring to do all His will. When I fail to be all that He would enable me to be, I will be sincere in repentance. I will cling to His merciful kindness in promising forgiveness of sin through the shed blood of our Lord and Savior Jesus Christ. By His grace, I will walk softly with a sincere heart. God is all I need in time of sorrow for sin. He is the only way of healing and peace.

The apostle Paul confessed this outworking of the old nature in his own life. He said that in his mind he served God, but in his flesh he sinned.

> *I delight in the law of God after the inward man:*
> *but I see another law in my members,*
> *warring against the law of my mind. . . .*
> *O wretched man that I am!*
> *who shall deliver me from the body of this death?*
> *I thank God through Jesus Christ our Lord.*
> *So then with the mind I myself serve the law of God;*
> *but with the flesh the law of sin.*
> ROMANS 7:22–25

God had said that dogs would lick the blood of King Ahab. The king soon proclaimed war against the Syrians, though God had expressly commanded him not to. Micaiah, God's prophet, had warned him that he would be soundly defeated. They went to battle anyway, a battle that not only brought defeat, but also a stray arrow that entered the king's chariot and proved to be God's tool for ending Ahab's wicked life on earth. As had been foretold, dogs licked his blood. What a bitter end to a wasted life! There comes a time in God's plan when it is too late.

—✺—

37

PROPHET OF FIRE

2 KINGS 1

Elijah had not died, because God was holding a secret concerning His faithful prophet. How secure it feels to realize that my times are in God's hand! He has eternally had a plan for me, knowing the perfect time for my leaving this world, just as He arranged my entering the world through physical birth.

About two years after Ahab humbled himself, God once again spoke to Elijah. The angel of the LORD came to Elijah and sent him on an errand of prophetic warning to King Ahaziah of Israel, son of King Ahab. It is not surprising to learn that, though the name Ahaziah means "Jehovah possesses," this son of Ahab walked in the way of his father and mother.

The king was ill after a fall from a lattice in his

upper chamber, and God told Elijah to bear news to the king that he would not recover. He would die. The king, however, had sent messengers to inquire of Baal-zebub about his recovery. Evidently, the worship of Baal gods still thrived in Samaria. Elijah met those messengers of the king and sent God's word to King Ahaziah through them.

Here we have a few words of description of the LORD's prophet. He was "an hairy man, and girt with a girdle of leather about his loins" (2 Kings 1:8). Here he is also again referred to as "Elijah the Tishbite." Elijah had been called the prophet of fire and, as at Mount Carmel, God would use him to bring fire down from heaven two more times.

Receiving the message, the king exercised his royal authority, sending a captain and his fifty men to Elijah to tell him to come down from the hill upon which he sat. Elijah, undaunted, responded, "If I be a man of God, then let fire come down from heaven, and consume thee and thy fifty" (2 Kings 1:10). God sent the fire to do just that.

The king sent a second captain with his fifty, and the message he brought to Elijah was to come down quickly! The previous scene was repeated, with God's fire from heaven consuming all fifty-one.

A third captain with fifty men was sent, but he came humbly, requesting the sparing of his life and the lives of his men. The angel of the LORD told

Elijah to go with him to the king without fear. It would be another opportunity for Elijah to stand boldly and speak to a king in the name of the LORD God of Israel.

Elijah went with the captain without fear, as he was directed. He pronounced the king's doom, "Thou shalt not come down off that bed on which thou art gone up, but shalt surely die" (2 Kings 1:16).

King Ahaziah died as God had said through Elijah, His faithful prophet.

And the sons of the prophets that were at Jericho came to Elisha, and said unto him, Knowest thou that the LORD will take away thy master from thy head to day? And he answered, Yea, I know it; hold ye your peace. And Elijah said unto him, Tarry, I pray thee, here; for the LORD hath sent me to Jordan. And he said, As the LORD liveth, and as thy soul liveth, I will not leave thee. And they two went on. And fifty men of the sons of the prophets went, and stood to view afar off: and they two stood by Jordan. And Elijah took his mantle, and wrapped it together, and smote the waters, and they were divided hither and thither, so that they two went over on dry ground.

And it came to pass, when they were gone over, that Elijah said unto Elisha, Ask what I shall do for thee, before I be taken away from thee. And Elisha said, I pray thee, let a double portion of thy spirit be upon me.

And he said, Thou hast asked a hard thing: nevertheless, if thou see me when I am taken from thee, it shall be so unto thee; but if not, it shall not be so.

And it came to pass, as they still went on, and talked, that, behold, there appeared a chariot of fire, and horses of fire, and parted them both asunder; and Elijah went up by a whirlwind into heaven. And Elisha saw it, and he cried, My father, my father, the chariot of Israel, and the horsemen thereof. And he saw him no more: and he took hold of his own clothes, and rent them in two pieces. He took up also the mantle of Elijah that fell from him, and went back, and stood by the bank of Jordan; and he took the mantle of Elijah that fell from him, and smote the waters, and said, Where is the LORD God of Elijah? and when he also had smitten the waters, they parted hither and thither: and Elisha went over.

2 KINGS 2:5–14

38

WHERE IS THE GOD OF ELIJAH?

2 KINGS 2

God had chosen to let Elisha know the day his friend and mentor would be taken away from him. We are not told how, but he knew, and he determined not to let Elijah out of his sight as long as Elijah lived. So Elisha said, "I will not leave thee" when Elijah suggested, "Tarry here. . .for the LORD hath sent me to Beth-el."

The two went to Bethel, Jericho, then Jordan. At the Jordan River, Elijah took his mantle and, wrapping it tightly to make it almost like a rod, smote the river. The waters divided, even as God had done for Moses and the children of Israel in the Exodus. Elijah and Elisha crossed over.

Elijah was about to say good-bye to his best earthly friend, and he tried to prepare him. "Before I am taken away from you, what shall I do for you?" he asked. Since Elisha already knew they would be separated, he had a request prepared: "I pray thee, let a double portion of thy spirit be upon me." To the Hebrew people, it would be obvious that he was asking to be counted as heir and successor, as the firstborn of the family.

Then came the chariot of fire, complete with horses of fire, parting the two and taking Elijah directly up into heaven by a whirlwind. Elisha saw it!

Elijah's translation into heaven is an Old Testament picture of our hope as New Testament believers. If I die, it will be only a passing through—God's whirlwind that will lift me from death's dark night into God's eternal light.

It is not a fact that I must die! Those of us yet living at the time Jesus returns will go up in the clouds to meet Him in the air! He will not send a chariot for us, but the Son of God personally will come and receive us unto Himself!

God's word says we will be caught up *together!* Isn't that a comforting word? No separations, no weeping, no heartaches forever—only together with our Lord and Savior, at home with our heavenly Father. Frailty, disease, and death will be left behind, and we will live forever in our glorified bodies, made perfectly whole and like our Savior Jesus Christ's. Jesus may come today!

Elisha saw Elijah no more. In grief, he tore his

clothes into two pieces. I wonder if it was with tears that he cried, "My father, my father!"

Then Elisha caught Elijah's mantle, which had been dropped as Elijah went up. Elisha took that mantle and with it hit the water of the Jordan River. He asked, "Where is the God of Elijah?" God was there, still the same God of power as He had always been for Elijah. The waters parted to allow Elisha to cross to the other side.

Elijah, his best friend and spiritual teacher, was gone, but God was just the same as He ever is—present, powerful, and providing all he needed. God hears the heart cry of His children and cares when they hurt. He tenderly comforts and gives grace and strength and desire to go on day after day in His will.

Where is the God of Elijah? Whenever, wherever, however I need Him, He is always present with me to provide all I have needed.

PART 4

"...AND SO MUCH MORE!"

ROMANS 5:9–10, 15, 17; MATTHEW 24:6

Much more then, being now justified by his blood,
we shall be saved from wrath through him.
For if, when we were enemies,
we were reconciled to God by the death of his Son,
much more, being reconciled,
we shall be saved by his life. . . .
For if through the offence of one many be dead,
much more the grace of God,
and the gift by grace, which is by one man,
Jesus Christ, hath abounded unto many. . . .
Much more they which receive abundance of grace
and of the gift of righteousness shall reign
in life by one, Jesus Christ.
ROMANS 5:9–10, 15, 17

39

JUST THE SAME TODAY

The God who lived on earth, worked miracles, cared about individuals, never failed, is just the same today!

"Lord, I need this. . .and this. . .and. . ."

How often I come to God and tell Him what I need. Sometimes I tell Him over and over. Yet I know before I ever speak that He knows and will provide. He has done so since eternity past—cared for everything He made. In eternity He planned to make me and to care for me all the days of this life and forever.

Even as I write, I am amazed at this truth. There is no question but that it is true. It is simply that the truth of eternity is infinitely high, far beyond the comprehension of my finite mind. I was made and live in time; how could I understand duration without beginning or end?

God has told me in His Word what I need to know: He is the Lord who changes not. He is faithful now and forever, with no lapse. In His everlasting love, God faithfully supplies all I need. Oh, how great is His faithfulness!

Trust in the LORD, and do good;
dwell in the land, and feed on His faithfulness.
PSALM 37:3 NKJV

He is always available, my security. He is my sustenance, my very life. As a wise parent, He gives good food suitable to His child's ability to chew and digest—just what I need, always sufficient to satisfy. The support of His arms is ever underneath, stabilizing my walk of faith. Oh, how sweet it is to trust in Jesus!

Yes, God has, moment by moment, provided all I have needed—and so much more! His bountiful love is expressed to me constantly in everyday ways.

I have found peace within and a confidence that God is in control and is maintaining my cause. This is easy when the winds of life softly whisper. But when the gale sweeps in with a blow that knocks the props out from under me, I have been profoundly impressed by God's audible words of peace in my heart. His power tangibly strengthened my inner being, as well as my physical being. He reminded me, "It is I: be not afraid." He gave grace to accept the "dangling" feeling, wondering what I can or should do next, fearing that I can't make it through this, dreading to face a life that will never be quite the same commodious one to which I have become accustomed.

I just now dumped dry cereal into my bowl of ice-cold milk, but before the bowl was full, I found that I could not get any more cereal out of that box.

Life is like that—full of surprises, some pleasant, many poignant. I had already eaten enough cereal. I wasn't hungry. I didn't need more calories, but would have munched anyway. So it was good that the box turned up empty. God provided exactly what I most needed—control. Yes, it was enforced self-control, but that was all I needed.

If the Lord Jesus does not come in the clouds today and take us out of here and into God's immediate presence, I will expect God's perfect care of me to continue for the duration. When God gives, I will find that I always possess all I have needed, and so much more!

Giant footsteps of fear tromp across my mind
And I worry, tremble, and dread:
The way appears formidable
When I can't see what's ahead.
But God's omnipotent goings,
Of tranquil, unwavering tread,
Banish my fears and uncertainties
And I confidently follow where He's led.

Dread not, neither be afraid of them.
The LORD your God which goeth before you,
he shall fight for you. . . .
DEUTERONOMY 1:29–30

For the LORD thy God hath blessed thee. . .
he knoweth thy walking through
this great wilderness. . .
the LORD thy God hath been with thee;
thou hast lacked nothing.
DEUTERONOMY 2:7

40

As If I Needed To

See that ye be not troubled.
MATTHEW 24:6

L ord, this morning I am worrying.
    It is as if I do not count as relevant the fact
that I have a Father who is omnipotent, omni-
scient, omnipresent, and omnilove.

I am worrying, not about today, but about
some other day that may be ahead, a day that may
be very difficult for me. Yet I do not even know if
I shall see the evening fall today.

But the evening will still fall, for You promised, in Genesis 8:22, day and night shall not cease
while the earth remains.

I also know You, the LORD God of heaven and
earth. I know You are my God. I know my times
are in Your hand (Psalm 31:15).

What else could I possibly need? How presump-
tuous am I not to trust You fully!

As if I could control my own future.
As if I needed to.

Surely goodness and mercy shall follow me
all the days of my life:
and I will dwell in the
house of the LORD for ever.
PSALM 23:6

ALL I HAVE NEEDED:
GOD

—⚊⚊—

Inspirational Library

Beautiful purse/pocket-size editions of Christian classics bound in flexible leatherette. These books make thoughtful gifts for everyone on your list, including yourself!

When I'm on My Knees   The highly popular collection of devotional thoughts on prayer, especially for women.
     Flexible Leatherette $4.97

The Bible Promise Book   Over 1,000 promises from God's word arranged by topic. What does God promise about matters like: Anger, Illness, Jealousy, Love, Money, Old Age, and Mercy? Find out in this book!
     Flexible Leatherette $3.97

Daily Wisdom for Women   A daily devotional for women seeking biblical wisdom to apply to their lives. Scripture taken from the New American Standard Version of the Bible.
     Flexible Leatherette $4.97

My Daily Prayer Journal   Each page is dated and features a Scripture verse and ample room for you to record your thoughts, prayers, and praises. One page for each day of the year.
     Flexible Leatherette $4.97

Available wherever books are sold.
Or order from:

Barbour Publishing, Inc.
P.O. Box 719
Uhrichsville, OH 44683
http://www.barbourbooks.com

If you order by mail, add $2.00 to your order for shipping.
Prices are subject to change without notice.